ETHNICITY AND EDUCATIONAL ACHIEVEMENT IN BRITISH SCHOOLS

Gajendra K. Verma

with

Brandon Ashworth

assisted by

Chris Bagley, Kanka Mallick, Tony Neasham

Foreword by Lord Swann, FRS, FRSE

M

MACMILLAN

First published 1986

Published by
THE MACMILLAN PRESS LTD
Houndmills, Basingstoke, Hampshire RG21 2XS
and London
Companies and representatives
throughout the world

Typeset by
Wessex Typesetters (Division of The Eastern Press Ltd)
Frome, Somerset

Printed in Great Britain by
Camelot Press Ltd
Southampton

British Library Cataloguing in Publication Data
Verma, Gajendra K.
Ethnicity and educational achievement in
British schools.
1. Minorities—Education—Great Britain
2. Academic achievement
I. Title II. Ashworth, Brandon
371.97′00941   LC3736.G6
ISBN 0–333–38549–7 (hardcover)
ISBN 0–333–38550–0 (paperback)

ETHNICITY AND EDUCATIONAL ACHIEVEMENT IN BRITISH SCHOOLS

Contents

Foreword

I first met Gajendra Verma in 1981, when I became Chairman of the Committee of Inquiry into the Education of Children from Ethnic Minority Groups. I soon realised the value of having, as one of our members, an academic whose own area of research fell four-square within the Committee's concerns, and a man, moreover, who himself comes from an Ethnic Minority. The Committee as a whole, and I personally, owe much to him, and it is with great pleasure that I write this brief Foreword to his latest book.

I joined the Committee as an almost complete newcomer to the problems with which we were to wrestle for some four years. But I soon discovered that many people who gave evidence to us, and even some members of the Committee, clung tenaciously to simple generalisations, and were determined to find, if they possibly could, a single cause for educational under-achievement – usually blaming it solely on 'racism in schools', or more particularly on teacher stereotypes.

It seemed to me, from the word go, that things could hardly be so simple. As a scientist, I am perhaps attuned to the idea that nothing is simple, even in the world of the physical sciences. And as someone who has spent much of his later life in the world of affairs, I am quite certain that the social sciences are a lot more complicated and difficult than the natural sciences. Quite soon, therefore, I started looking at the whole range of factors that were likely to be involved in human situations where children from widely differing cultures were mixed up together, in a society that had previously been substantially homogeneous.

Needless to say, there are a great many relevant factors. Socio-economic status has long been known to relate closely to educational achievement, though the interplay of cause and effect is by no means wholly clear. And it has become very obvious in recent years that racial prejudice and discrimination do much to lower socio-economic status in many minority groups. Children's immediate environment, in the classroom, with their peers, with their family, and in their community, must be important. So must the individual child's own psychological make-up. And running through this multiplicity of factors, must be the widely differing cultural backgrounds of Britain's many minority groups, and their diverse reactions to the prejudice and discrimination to which so many of them are subjected. To imagine that only one of these many factors leads to poor achievement strains credulity to the limit. It is, of course, far more likely that all of them are involved, in various ways, and in varying degrees.

The Committee's Final Report by no means succeeded in disentangling this complex web of factors, though I believe it went some way to doing so. In its chapter on Achievement and Underachievement and elsewhere, mention is to be found of all the points I have listed above, though all too often only brief mention. In part this is due to lack of hard evidence, but in part, it has to be said, and now that the Report is published it can be said, it is due to a general reluctance to examine the more politically sensitive areas.

Dr Verma's book, it should be said, does not shy off such matters, and it incorporates some valuable research that he carried out for the Committee, at rather short notice, following widespread resistance, in some circles, to a very major research project that the Committee had commissioned. This, we had hoped, would examine the factors – in school, at home and in the community – that led to success (and lack of success) amongst white children, West Indian children, and Asian children. Dr Verma's work for the Committee goes some way to making good this loss.

His book has a number of striking features. It is elegantly and clearly written – something that is refreshing, and unexpected in the research literature of educational psychology. He handles sensitive matters with a sympathy that is broad and clear. He makes no bones about the inadequacies of the relevant research, including his own. But above all, the book is suffused with a realisation of the complexities of the matters in question, and a determination not to be led anywhere near to the 'fallacy of the single cause'.

In consequence this is a book to be read, and read with care; for the general perspective that it provides, for the conclusions that it draws, and above all for the avenues it explores.

LORD SWANN, FRS, FRSE

Preface

The research reported in this book was conducted in three phases during the period October 1977 to July 1983, and was based at the University of Bradford. The first phase was designed to explore the possible determinants of the vocational aspirations, choices and achievements of ethnic minority adolescents in the Leeds/Bradford area of West Yorkshire, England. The second phase examined the occupational experience of a cohort of adolescents, a large proportion of whom came from the various ethnic minority groups; it attempted to set this experience in the context of achievement aspirations, educational achievement and expectations of working life. The final phase was concerned with the educational achievement of ethnic minority adolescents. It was hoped to establish profiles of high and low achievers among adolescents within different ethnic groups.

The primary intention, derived from three linked research programmes, was to gain insight into educational, social, cultural and psychological processes which contribute to educational achievement for various ethnic groups in British schools. These processes represent complex interactions of many factors and it was necessary therefore to develop a model to clarify how each factor might operate within the whole process. The model allowed for three levels of analysis:

(a) the broad socio-economic or macro considerations, and in particular ethnicity;
(b) the 'immediate environment', which concerns the school, peer-group and family experiences of the individual;
(c) the individual himself/herself and the psychological concepts through which certain achievement levels may be mediated.

Before examination of the model employed in the study a brief description of what has been presumed to be 'ethnicity' and 'educational achievement' is offered. These terms do not have the same meaning for all those concerned with the educational process, particularly in a culturally pluralist society. The research has adopted a multidisciplinary approach. No claim is made for comprehensiveness since the literature of the area is extensive. However, it was possible to derive a new insight from reviews and discussions of various views and research findings into differential achievement of pupils belonging to different ethnic groups.

The final text was written by Gajendra K. Verma. It embodies the prejudices, biases and obsessions of the senior author, and he must assume primary responsibility for the way the book is received and for its merits and defects.

Gajendra K. Verma was responsible for directing the three research projects; Peter Sanderson was research assistant on the first project and Brandon Ashworth and Teresa Brown worked as research assistants on the second and third projects – Brandon Ashworth being responsible for the analysis of psychometric data. Chris Bagley was a consultant on all phases of the work.

It is hoped that the findings presented in this book will be accessible to teachers, teacher trainers, educational decision-makers, parents and others interested in and responsible for the education of all pupils, especially those from ethnic minority groups.

Finally, we believe that an impetus for changes in the structure of education must come through the contribution of researchers seeking insights into the forces at work in equality of educational achievement and equality of outcome.

University of Manchester   GAJENDRA K. VERMA

Acknowledgements

In a longitudinal study one is conscious of the fact that many people have provided support, information and assistance at different stages of the research over six years.

We are grateful to nine schools in the Leeds/Bradford area which formed the nucleus of the research. Because of the demands of confidentiality no schools, headteachers, teachers or careers advisers can be named or adequately thanked publicly. However, without their generous help in terms of time and information provided it would have been impossible to accomplish this work. Throughout the field work they allowed us unlimited access to all aspects of their institutional life. The youngsters who participated in this research deserve a very special word of appreciation and admiration for their tolerance and serendipity which make empirical research so stimulating and thought-provoking. Our appreciation also goes to the parents of those youngsters for allowing their children to be exposed to the scrutiny of the researchers.

We would like to thank the Leverhulme Trust Fund for providing the financial support for the first stage of the research (1977–79), the Nuffield Foundation for the second stage of the research (1980–82), and the Department of Education and Science and the Rowntree Trust for the third stage (1982–83).

We would like to express our gratitude to the following for their valuable contributions to the book: Tony Neasham, Leslie Woodcock and Chris Bagley who read the complete manuscript and offered ideas and criticism in numerous and helpful ways which led me to rewrite certain sections; Kanka Mallick for reading and commenting on the manuscript; Emeritus Professor Ruth Beard for the willingness to give generously her time and wisdom for discussion during the first two stages of the research. In addition to those mentioned above, many others have contributed to the collection of research data at one stage or another and we wish to acknowledge their support.

We would like to thank Bridget Wilkie and Chloe Gainham who typed the several drafts of the manuscript with great speed, accuracy and patience. The authors, however, bear full responsibility for the final product.

1 Introduction

Education is a topic almost constantly in the news. This is hardly surprising since it impinges on our lives in many different ways, whether we be pupil, student, parent, member of the older generation, tax-payer or rate-payer. As a result most of us place a good deal of faith, even blind faith, in education. Education is also intimately connected with the problems of plural societies. Studies in Britain and America have shown that education, especially intercultural education, has a marked effect on the social and personal development of the individual. Writing about the basic premise of intercultural education Allport (1958) remarked that 'no person knows his own culture who knows only his own culture'. But let us not pretend that all the problems of individual development in a plural society can be solved by education alone. There are other forces which create strains and anxieties and may seriously affect the development of an individual; one of these is the kind of structural and social systems in which people live.

However, it is clear that the role of formal education in the increasing technological complexity and inter-dependence of modern societies is undoubtedly an important one. Access to education, once for a small privileged section of the population, is now a basic 'right' for all. In most developed societies children are required to undergo a stipulated minimum period of compulsory schooling. As societies have become more complex, greater reliance has been placed in formal educational structures, going beyond those of compulsory schooling into those of further education. As a result, the educational system is constantly subject to pressures – both internal and external – arising from the diversity of often competing demands that society makes upon the system. Public concern is expressed as to quality and cost; this concern is the most persistent theme of those who seek new forms of accountability. They argue that standards are slipping or that the learning experiences offered by institutions are not keeping pace with the requirements of a society beset by industrial imperatives.

There is also concern as to the usefulness of existing educational provision to the individual and to society as a whole; there is concern about the returns on public investment in education made by national and local government, quite apart from any personal sacrifices made to help individuals maximise their educational opportunities.

One of the many strands in the argument that surrounds education is that of the adequacy of existing provision to a particular child or type of child. One such type is the 'ethnic minority child'; others include the 'inner city child', the 'gifted child' and the 'handicapped child'. While labels tend to reduce children to ciphers and to discount the uniqueness of the individual's experience, such categorisation is perhaps an inevitable consequence of seeking to focus on a particular facet of educational provision. That type of focus is nevertheless consistent with the terms of the British 1944 Education Act which marked the beginning of the operationalisation of the ideal of providing education for each child 'according to its age, aptitude and ability'.

The aims of formal education vary in emphasis from society to society. Broadly speaking, they serve two inter-related functions. The first of these centres on the individual. Education seeks to foster an individual's development in terms of the acquisition of skills and knowledge valued by that society. These range from the basics of literacy and numeracy to the more sophisticated ones that will enable a particular career path or channel of employment to be followed.

The second function centres on the needs and requirements of society as a whole if it is to operate effectively. The dominant idelogies of that society will determine the conception of those needs and requirements, and the resources that are to be made available to operate the educational system. An elaborate system of rewards – in terms of wealth and/or status – is offered, commensurate with the proficiency acquired in particular levels of skills considered necessary for the effective functioning of that society. The dominant culture will also determine the degree of freedom of access to acquire particular skills, thus establishing a particular societal hierarchy.

Embracing these two inter-related functions there is a further purpose behind education, one which is also subject to the dominant ideologies of the particular society. This formalises and extends the patterns of socialisation developed in the child by the home. These patterns set models for behaviour in group settings in the school and ultimately in the world of work and the wider social setting. They include a conception of membership of that society, the particular identity which it seeks to justify. At the explicit level this process may well involve the training of the individual to conform to the 'norms' or 'rules' of that society; at the implicit level, the information and values utilised in the instilling of the skills and knowledge (and reflecting the cultural assumptions of that society) will influence the behaviour of the individual towards other people. In a sense, therefore, formal education, while attempting to meet the present and future needs of society, nonetheless perpetuates the past. Thus education is a powerful force in moulding the individual and the society it serves.

One of the axioms of modern societies, particularly the so-called democratic ones, is 'equality of opportunity'. This implies that, theoretically at least, the chances of personal advancement in terms of education, wealth, social status and power within that society should be the same for all, regardless of the individual's background, gender, ethnicity and race. This idea of 'equality of opportunity' came to prominence in American political debate in the 1960s, but is a deep-rooted idea in bourgeois, liberal society. It is indeed functional for such a society if all the runners in the race of life start as equals; but the institutional processes of discrimination which influence outcome are hardly addressed by this principle.

A more radical and far-reaching concept is that of 'equality of achievement', which emerged in the debate on structural discrimination in American society in the 1970s (Lewis, 1978). This concept, which has equal applicability to British society, argues that principles of social justice require that all social groups in society, however defined (by religion, class of origin, gender, culture or ethnicity) should on average have *equal* levels of achievement. This is indeed a radical conception, for it implies that society should diminish and finally eradicate all the negative influences upon educational achievement imposed by economic and social disadvantage. There may be various ways of doing this; but diminishing social class differences is the most radical strategy.

The concept of 'equality of achievement' is an important principle for consideration in the debate about ethnicity and achievement. It is also an important focal point, particularly in a democratic society, in the debate and dialogue about the role and values of formal education and its accessibility to all sections of the population.

PLURALISM AND EDUCATION IN BRITAIN

In many Western countries the emerging 'pluralist' composition of society has been in recent years a matter of debate. It has arisen out of the demographic, social and cultural changes brought about by post-war migration. There have been, and continue to be, discussion and arguments arising out of attempts to characterise or analyse the nature of particular societies.

The idea of 'pluralism' grew out of the work of sociologists and political scientists who described the cultural and institutional separateness of ethnic groups in some third world countries (such as Burma, Guyana and Jamaica). The idea of pluralism has been more recently applied in the European context to societies such as the Netherlands, which has a long history of the plural or institutional separateness of religious and political groups (Bagley, 1973).

Two types of pluralism have been identified. The first, political pluralism, refers to profound ideological differences (political or religious) in a society which is otherwise culturally and ethnically homogeneous – traditional Dutch society is an example of such political pluralism (Bagley, 1973). The second type, cultural pluralism, is marked by institutional and value separateness of ethnic and linguistic groups within the same society – examples of cultural pluralism can be found in both Canada and the United States (Appleton, 1983). A central defining factor of both types of pluralism is that the different plural groups or blocs in society have relatively equal power and equal access to crucial economic and social resources. Essentially too, the different plural groups in the society should have a shared commitment to the overriding goals of society, and agreement about the role of the state in supporting different plural groups in maintaining their cultural and .political autonomy. The official Canadian policy of multiculturalism, providing generous state support through a common political consensus for cultural retention by some 80 officially defined cultural or ethnic groups is a good example of this.

It hardly needs to be said that Britain is not yet a plural society. Some attempts have been made at plural accommodation in Ulster, but the great imbalances of power between the two religious groupings still remain. The pressures on ethnic minority groups in Britain range from assimilation to threats of exclusion (the true mark of racism). Cultural pluralism in the sense defined by Appleton (1983) does not prevail in Britain. Indeed, a movement towards geographical and cultural cohesion in ghetto-like circumstances, a kind of pseudo-pluralism, is a fundamentally racist solution to problems of ethnic minorities in Britain. Mullard (1981) refers to such pressures as ethnicism, a new form of racism through which 'ethclasses' are embedded within traditional social class groupings, leaving traditional stratification patterns unchallenged.

The fundamental challenge of the struggle to reach equality of achievement by the new ethnic groups in Britain may or may not lead to true pluralism; but what should be challenged in this process is the structure of equality, the traditional patterning of social disadvantage, and the nature of the class system itself.

A major part of the debate around the issue of equality and ethnicity has centred on education. As a key social institution, the school has a major role to play, on the one hand in promoting individual self-development, and on the other, in preparing individuals to meet the needs and requirements of society. Education might find it easier to achieve these twin aims if children came from similar socio-economic, cultural, religious and linguistic backgrounds. In a multi-ethnic society however, the population is composed of a number of distinguishable ethnic groups and this inevitably affects the process of education.

Ethnic minority children – although not a new phenomenon in British schooling – came to feature in classrooms, as their numbers increased in the wake of post-war migration to this country. It brought many people from the New Commonwealth (e.g. the Caribbean, Africa, India, Bangladesh, Pakistan and South East Asia). This population of migrants is not homogeneous and came from many parts of the New Commonwealth. Despite this, policy makers and politicians have approached 'ethnicity' in an over-inclusive and often stereotyped way.

Education has faced the challenge of a new reality because of the growing ethnic diversity of the school population, and the resultant need for an appropriate response. At first provision for ethnic minority children in the classroom consisted primarily of equipping them to cope with life in British society; for some of these children provision centred on teaching them English.

The debate concerning the formal education of ethnic minority pupils in British society has centred for a number of years around the issues of language and dialect, race relations, ethnicity, religion, achievement and disadvantage. The fundamental philosophy at the initial stages was the smooth absorption of ethnic minorities into the mainstream educational system. The 'culture' of ethnic minorities was regarded as a handicap to this process.

Among the educational policies and practices adopted to deal with the needs of ethnic minorities have been those concerned with compensatory measures, designed to counteract disadvantage. This approach has proved to be inadequate for two reasons. First, all too often sincere intentions behind compensatory programmes to offset disadvantage have misguided those concerned about equality of achievement. As a result, the thrust of various programmes has been on the so-called 'deficiencies' of ethnic minority groups, and has thus tended to reinforce the notions that these groups were somehow 'inferior'. Secondly, despite its desirability, equality of achievement is not easily attained, given the subordinate role of education as a system of differentiation and classification of the workforce in an advanced industrial society such as Britain (Halsey and Goldthorpe, 1980).

In order to reach some understanding of the implications of such issues in terms of the present day needs and challenges facing schools in Britain, it is necessary to look at the various views and ideologies which thread their way through the history of the past thirty years. The approaches and strategies, in many cases conflicting ones, designed to meet those needs and challenges can be broadly categorised as assimilationist; integrationist; and multicultural/anti-racist education.

In the 1960s the only explicit principle was that the new ethnic/cultural groups in Britain would 'merge' with the relatively homogeneous existing population just as it was thought that previous groups of immigrants had been assimilated. This merging has been described as 'assimilation', though the implications of this practice were neither closely defined nor challenged at the time. The Department of Education and Science (then called the Ministry of Education) took only cautious steps towards establishing a policy on the education of ethnic minority groups and most of the actions are now openly criticised. Willey (1982) comments that:

> Initial central government reaction to immigration . . . in the 1950s and early 1960s was to play down the implications, to suggest that no particular social policy response – or action by teachers – was necessary.

However, many urban schools had already been attempting for some time to provide special programmes for ethnic minority pupils, without any guidance from the then Ministry of Education.

At first educational provisions were very much 'ad hoc', and the main emphasis was on compensatory programmes such as the teaching of English. The acquisition of English was perceived as the key to cultural and social assimilation. The educational system responded with what were considered as appropriate provisions; language centres, language units, peripatetic teaching of English as a second language and the system of 'withdrawal' came into operation. Schools with ethnic minority pupils saw, however symbolically and stereotypically, 'non-English-speaking children' (particularly Asians) as a 'major problem' and the solution was for them to acquire English. Thus, some of the schools' proudest achievements in the language field and in acquainting ethnic minority children about the British way of life came to be labelled as assimilationist, and hence racist; because it was argued that they denied implicitly the validity of positive aspects of the ethnic minority cultures. Furthermore, the fact that schools were unaware of the language needs of West Indian children was an obvious fault in teaching policy and practices. It should also be recalled that the main impulse behind most of the changes was parochial. The national response was, and still is, lacking in vision.

As the number of ethnic minority pupils increased in some LEAs, other measures were felt necessary. For example, in June 1965, at the initiative of the DES a minority of the then 64 Local Education Authorities with a significant proportion of children from New Commonwealth backgrounds (usually of South Asian origin) adopted a 'bussing' policy. Its implementation meant that ethnic minority pupils of all ages were transported every day from where they lived, to attend a more distant school. Such a practice clearly reflected the ideology of the time, namely to seek to assimilate different ethnic/cultural groups within the mainstream of society. The impact of such a policy on educational practice would supposedly be to make these ethnic minority children as 'British' as their white counterparts. In recent years, many writers (e.g. Street-Porter, 1978; Willey, 1982) have criticised such policies as ethnocentric, reinforcing the dominant culture, and indeed as racist. The practice of dispersal had come under attack on social, psychological and educational grounds as well. The policy of dispersal was abandoned.

The growth in the number of black and Asian children in schools, it was felt, necessitated a radical approach. People giving evidence to the Parliamentary Select Committee in 1973 maintained that the presence of ethnic minorities had implications for all schools whatever their ethnic/cultural composition. In the early 1970s there began a shift in thinking away from 'assimilation' towards 'integration'. It was advocated that educational practice should aim to promote unity within the wider society while at the same time allowing for diversity among the various component groups. Such a policy would entail designing educational programmes to meet the perceived special needs and aspirations of ethnic minority pupils. Research conducted during this period shows that the education of ethnic minorities was perceived as 'problem oriented' (Verma and Bagley, 1979). Perhaps a parallel could be traced in the evolving philosophy of comprehensive education, away from the naive conception of 'grammar school education for all' towards the realisation that education should recognise the differences among children and meet the needs of the individual. Thus it was moving away from the conception that education should seek to fit children into particular moulds.

The integrationist approach has not been without its critics. It has been dubbed as a subtle form of racism directed at the cultures and life-styles of ethnic minorities which provided a challenge to traditional British practices and beliefs (Mullard, 1981; Stone, 1981). It was also recognised that the ability to tolerate diversity in schools required teachers to have an understanding of the social, religious, linguistic and cultural backgrounds of all children. Unfortunately, many teacher training institutions have not yet felt the need to redesign the curriculum to meet the needs and challenges posed by the changed characteristics of British society.

In the 1980s more diverse views of society prevail than during the last two decades. There is now much resistance to the simplistic ideas of 'assimilation' and 'integration' which pervaded much official thinking in the 1960s and 1970s. Although some educators still subscribe to the earlier school of thought (and the rejectionist view also survives), the idea of cultural pluralism reflected in multicultural education is now gaining ground in Britain.

The perspective of cultural pluralism, often confused with multiculturalism, recognises the need of each ethnic group to develop and retain its distinct culture and traditions within a political framework involving dynamic relationships with the other ethnic groups that make up the wider society. Central to cultural pluralism is the need for a climate in which people from the ethnic minorities, either as individuals or groups, are able to participate fully in the life of the nation without detriment to their ethnic values, beliefs, practices and loyalties.

Pluralism in practice means that different cultural and ethnic groups in the same society not merely exist side by side, but understand sympathetically each other's folkways, life-styles, literature, customs, and aspirations. Triandis (1976) rightly argues that:

Integration which is mere contact between two groups is held to be potentially counterproductive as a remedy for the inequality seen between blacks and whites, an inequality consequent to persisting exploitation by the majority of the minority group. A three-pronged strategy to achieve *additive multiculturalism*, an essential step forward to a pluralist society, is advocated. The development of interdependence, appreciation, and the skills to interact intimately with persons from other cultures are the requirements laid down. (p. 179)

The British government at last declared its position about multiculturalism (a possible prelude to true cultural pluralism) in the 1977 Green Paper 'Education in Schools'. This Paper not only emphasised that the presence of ethnic minority pupils in Britain had implications for the education of all children, but that all schools, whatever their ethnic composition, should give their pupils an understanding both of the multi-ethnic nature of British society and of Britain's place in the interdependent world. The Green Paper refers to 'the needs of this new Britain' which should be reflected in schools' curricula. Yet education authorities in areas where there are few minority pupils still believe in general that the wider multi-ethnic society has little relevance to their teaching practice (Little and Willey, 1981).

The core of this emerging model of cultural pluralism is that the different ethnic, cultural and religious groups making up society, ought to have equal power, in terms of access to economic and political resources. If such equality of power is not provided, ethnic differentiation in society becomes a form of racism rather than pluralism. The question arises as to whether society at large is ready to commit itself to cultural pluralism to the extent of including ethnic groups in the power structure.

A major difficulty in designing programmes for cultural pluralism is whether the focus should be on the life-styles or life-chances of ethnic minorities. Life-chances have to do with access to power and resources and equality of opportunity; but unfortunately most of the programmes are still geared towards life-styles. The underlying philosophy of such an approach appeals to liberal-minded people. Nevertheless, in the last few years many teachers and writers have begun to argue that the emphasis must shift from life-styles to the life-chances of all children.

The educational response to the presence of ethnic minority groups in British society can be seen as a movement through three overlapping phases based in turn upon the concepts of assimilation, integration and pluralism. Multiculturalism has evolved as a reaction to the previous two decades of educational policy and practice. The concept of multicultural education reflects a growing pluralist notion of society.

In a truly plural society, education should be appropriate to the needs and aspirations of all cultural/ethnic groups. In that sense 'multicultural education' is the logical and practical antecedent and extension of that idea of pluralism. It is assumed that such a strategy will provide a sound base from which ethnic minorities will be able to attain equality of achievement in the wider society. This model of multicultural education, based on the equal power of cultural and ethnic groups within a particular nation, is intrinsically attractive, and refreshingly innovative in its implications for the reform of British education and society (Verma and Bagley, 1984).

There are both proponents and critics of the concept and the practice of multicultural education. Perhaps the most optimistic view of multicultural education is that taken by the Rampton Report (HMSO, 1981, p. 71) which argued that 'a theory and practice of a multicultural approach to education' exists.

It is clear however from an examination of the many programmes, philosophies and strategies of 'multicultural education' in Britain that they are 'ad hoc' and, in their confusions and lack of balance, reflect competing claims for political, social and economic power. The educational system has so far failed to concern itself with the preparation of all individuals to live in a society composed of varied cultures, social norms and life-styles, but interdependent. It has failed also in its intentions of helping pupils to understand the nature of racism, and the gross inequalities of power in British society. There has been rhetorical commitment, at least, to the ideology that multicultural education – by changing the curriculum – will enhance equality of opportunity for pupils from minority communities and increase their life-chances. Critics point out that without coming to grips with the key issues of social and institutional changes, mere tinkering with the periphery of the curriculum will have little impact. Bullivant (1981), one of the strongest critics of multicultural education, argues that multicultural education could, in effect, be a strategy for controlling minorities, rather than enhancing their self-determination.

The problems and issues outlined concerning the education of all ethnic groups in Britain will not go away overnight. There is a great diversity of cultural, ethnic and social patterns in British society. Hence it is unlikely that one single model or approach will presently emerge to meet the needs and aspirations of all concerned. Multicultural education must allow for considerable variations within any context, since it is likely that some individuals are more 'ethnic' or culturally 'retentionist' than others. Social, cultural, linguistic, religious, socio-economic class and personal characteristics all contribute to the particular educational aspirations of ethnic groups, which can range from education for 'assimilation' to education for 'cultural autonomy'. This freedom of educational aspiration is qualified in a number of ways: any model adopted by the majority in any particular educational setting should allow for any individual in that situation to opt for a different model without sanction; the education should impart to the individual advanced cognitive skills for maximum cultural participation and upward social mobility; and the education should be fundamentally non-sexist and non-racist.

The ultimate aim of multicultural education must be to facilitate the social and scholastic development of young people who have a cognitively complex view of the world in which they live (Bagley and Verma, 1983). While it is right that they should retain a sense of pride in their personal and cultural identity, children of all ethnic groups should be able to acquire an empathetic awareness of others with differing personal and cultural identities. In effect what is proposed here is the development of a particular attitude or approach for individuals or groups which would ideally permeate the whole educational system (Verma, 1984).

Schools have a crucial role to play in attaining the aims of multicultural education, but other agencies also have a part in this process. The orientation of multicultural education must recognise that a range of alternative strategies exists within any society, and that it should be possible for young people to operate from a wide spectrum of interacting cultural bases (Verma, 1984).

Against that climate of change, this study reflects on one feature of pluralist education, namely that of the educational achievement of ethnic minority children in Britain. However desirable may be a particular educational climate in terms of a multicultural, pluralist or whatever orientation, the value of that orientation will be debased if the educational outcomes continue to lack credibility. If the potential and aspirations of the ethnic minority population are adversely met compared to those of the majority population, then equality of achievement will not be realised.

2   Race, Culture and Ethnicity

When looking at the process of educational achievement in a plural society, concepts that come readily to mind are 'race', 'culture' and 'ethnicity'. Of these, the most widely used are 'race' and 'culture'. Their use as concepts will be considered as a prelude to discussion of 'ethnicity' which is the latest one in the British context.

The concepts of 'race' and 'culture' are the subject of much confusion, as indeed is 'ethnicity' itself. This confusion which exists in the minds of many people is compounded by popular myth and by the varying applications which those terms have been given in the social sciences. Writers have approached the issues of ethnicity in the educational context from a variety of perspectives and ideologies, each with its own terminology (Verma, 1984).

THE LABEL OF 'RACE'

In the context of education, ethnicity, and cross-cultural research 'race' is the most widely used concept and perhaps the one most abused. Originally it was a biological concept designed to categorise people by their physical characteristics (e.g. colour of skin, texture of hair, shape of skull, nose or cheekbones). This notion led to three broad racial categories: Caucasian (including the large majority of people from the Indian sub-continent), Negroid and Mongoloid.

For explaining differences in human behaviour, such categories serve little purpose. Furthermore, there are various limitations in classifying people on the racial dimension. For example, people from the Indian sub-continent are sometimes regarded as a racial group distinct from the Caucasian one. Such explanations are invalid, because, except for the Aboriginal people and some of those in the North Western territories of India, the majority from that sub-continent are, strictly speaking, Caucasian. Yet few people would

12

deny that there are many attributes which make people from India distinctive in appearance and behaviour from, say, the English, who are also for the most part Caucasian.

Even if the Caucasian group, for example, is divided into sub-groups, the movement of people over centuries has further reduced the usefulness of race, in its biological sense, to explain human behaviour. Firstly, the division of human types into Caucasian, Negroid and Mongoloid is very much an arbitrary one with much blurring at the edges; for example there are East African and Indonesian people who live at the geographical margins of the 'homelands' of the traditional racial groups. Secondly, human migration has brought about a substantial dispersal of these types across the world. Thirdly, migration has also led to considerable inter-racial mixes as a result of marriage and other unions. Dyer (1974) has shown that the boundaries between traditional racial groupings are growing so blurred in terms of behaviour, culture and geography that in future centuries mixed-race ancestry will be the rule rather than the exception.

Quite apart from the complexities of inter-racial mixes over centuries, the use of the biologically-based term 'race' contributes very little to understanding human behaviour. Some writers disapprove of it even as an analytical term. There is evidence in the literature to show that the concept of 'race' is frequently over-generalised in ways which serve to reinforce traditional stereotypes (Banton, 1979). The term has acquired a popular meaning bearing little relationship to biological or anthropological reality.

'Race' has had all manner of attributes attached to it that transcend the narrow biological ones. Language, religion, mores, customs, dress-styles and other elements have become part of its meaning. In other words, it has come to be a socio-cultural metaphor, and one with unfortunate connotations. 'Race' is an unsatisfactory concept; neither in terms of its biological base nor of its metaphorical trappings does it offer a valid means of distinguishing between people. In this complex situation many people find it difficult to make a clear distinction between biological and cultural differences, and tend to associate one with the other. It must be recognised that biological and cultural differences are independent of each other. The concept of race, therefore, is not a meaningful tool in the search for answers to differential achievement amongst different ethnic groups. As Banton (1979) rightly comments: 'Whenever anyone is inclined to use the word "race" he should pause and wonder whether [there] is not another word that will help express his meaning more precisely. Usually there is.'

The way 'race' has been used not only to classify people but to denigrate certain groups of people takes us into the arena of racism. Just as misconceptions surround the use of 'race', racism itself confuses biological and cultural differences. When an ideological orientation is adopted that maintains that a particular group of people is *racially* superior to other groups, the situation is compounded. At the core of racist theory is the assertion that inequality is absolute and unconditional. Racism differentiates ideologically between groups of people, thus imposing a particular social definition upon them. Laferriere (1983) defines racism as 'the use of ascriptive, or quasi-ascriptive characteristics, and particularly of race, for the inferiorisation of and discrimination against certain categories of people.'

The modern myths and assumptions that serve to define and structure specific situations in terms of 'race' are attributes of racism. In today's society racism is prevalent on many levels. In 'functional' terms it seeks to suppress the rights of other people to enjoy similar freedoms to those of the 'dominant' group; usually the dominant group is white. Resting on notions of white superiority reinforced by the years and in some cases, centuries, of political and economic power it has wielded over others, the dominant group ruthlessly guards its privileges and advantages. The policies of apartheid practised in South Africa offer the most striking example of this. Those policies, built on the notions of white supremacy, seek to maintain the principles of separate development for the 'coloured' and 'black' members of its population. Despite constituting 90 per cent of the population, the coloureds and blacks still find their life-chances (educational, economic and social) firmly subordinated to those of the dominant white minority.

In some respects, the situation in many Western countries is not altogether dissimilar to that in South Africa, except in degree. Although they have no overt policy of apartheid, racism continues to depress the life-chances of ethnic minority people. These countries have attempted to tackle racist attitudes and behaviour through legislation and in various other ways. Nonetheless, racist behaviours, attitudes and beliefs still exist.

Such racism can be 'institutionalised', where government agencies, concerned with education, social welfare, employment, housing and so forth, operate intentionally or unintentionally against the best interests of certain sections of the population. It also occurs at the 'individual' level, where behaviours, attitudes and beliefs of individuals acting singly or collectively impair the life-chances and well-being of other individuals or groups that they see as different (and perhaps as inferior) to themselves. Much of the impetus for racism seems to be the legacy of the older notions of varying levels of racial capabilities and worthiness. Jencks (1972) succinctly summarises the global dynamics of racism:

As of 1972, white people still ran the world. Those who have power always prefer to believe that they 'deserve' it, rather than thinking they have won it by venality, cunning or historical accidents. Some whites apparently feel that if the average white is slightly more adept at certain kinds of abstract reasoning than the average black, this legitimises the whole structure of white supremacy – not just in America, but around the world. Conversely, many people seem to feel that if blacks and whites are born with the same capacity for abstract reasoning, this proves that white supremacy is illegitimate – and therefore perhaps temporary.

Finally, it should be mentioned that in some cross-cultural research racism finds its ideological justification in attempts to show that differences between groups are genetic in their origins. The views of Jensen (1969), Schockley (1972) and Eysenck (1971) amongst others, are clear examples of scientific racism.

THE CONCEPT OF CULTURE

The second concept to consider is 'culture'. In social science research and in popular usage, both 'culture' and 'race' have been subject to a variety of interpretations. As a result much confusion surrounds them. Even within the academic disciplines there is little agreement as to the nature of 'culture'.

While there is some common ground in that, whatever the precise usage given to the term, it tends to imply that individuals or groups of people 'belong to' or 'live in' a particular culture, this seems to be a simplistic view of culture, offering not much more than a superficial means of labelling people. In this sense it can be said that A is 'from the Indian culture'. However, this is a simplistic interpretation of an individual's complex attributes. In fact, people belong to social groups; they are born into a social group and acquire its characteristics. In this conceptualisation, culture encompasses almost every aspect of human development. Thus it is not simply the sum of all individuals within a social group, but an identity base to which any individual can subscribe.

Culture is not a static entity in the form of a fixed social heritage. It does not exist in a vacuum; it evolves and changes over time. Cultural changes are inevitable as long as there are contacts and competition between cultures (Arensberg and Niehoff, 1971). Today changes can be seen in many cultures, even in those considered as traditional ones, as a result of changes in political and economic systems and communications. Many traditional cultural characteristics disappear or change when they are no longer able to meet the challenge of social, economic and technological changes. This has bearing on the acculturation process, and ultimately mediates on the achievement process.

The heterogeneity of some social groups further complicates the picture. Regional characteristics, religion, occupation and socio-economic status all contribute to the formation of sub-cultures. Therefore, we do not expect only intercultural differences, but also intracultural differences, although intracultural differences should be smaller than intercultural ones. As Bullivant (1981) comments:

Culture can be thought of as the knowledge and conceptions embodied in symbolic and non-symbolic communication modes, about the technology and skills, customary behaviours, values, beliefs and attitudes, a society has evolved from its historical past and progressively modifies and augments to give meaning to and cope with the present and anticipated future problems of its existence.

The above perspective clearly suggests that culture should not be interpreted entirely in terms of a socio-biological, problem-solving, survival device in the ecological sense, although this aspect of human life is also important. Such a model of culture should also be seen in terms of the expressive aspect, bearing in mind that culture is past, present and future orientated.

A further point that should be considered is that cultures are not discrete entities. Particular values, attitudes and behaviours, for example, may be part of a number of cultures, although their relative importance may vary considerably from culture to culture. Thus, it could be said that intercultural differences are often ones of degree rather than absolute ones. This is a point we shall return to when ethnicity is discussed. Individuals, whatever their cultural backgrounds, are not merely 'cultural beings' but also 'social beings'. These aspects are inseparable. While culture influences individuals, individuals in turn contribute to culture through enriching or modifying it. Culture, therefore, should not be treated as an isolated, static or homogeneous phenomenon.

The concept of bi- or multi-cultural identity may seem to be the desirable goal in socialising all pupils in a plural society. Children brought up within two cultures, for example, South Asian and the dominant white British culture, may show greater flexibility in cognitive styles, adaptability and creativity. The norms of both cultural groups are assimilated and utilised by the child, depending upon the demands of the situation. There are obvious benefits if the child is socialised within more than one cultural group's norms. Such a bi-cultural child develops unique strength and flexibility by merging two styles. Taylor's (1976) study in England showed how young South Asians were becoming bi-cultural in a true sense, although because of the resistance on the part of a large section of the dominant culture, this model has not become fully functional in the British context.

WHAT IS ETHNICITY?

The discussion of 'race' and 'culture' shows that neither is adequate for the analysis and understanding of educational issues in a plural society; the concept of ethnicity seems more appropriate.

Analysis of the term 'ethnicity' has been approached in a variety of ways in the social sciences. This is reflected in the range of definitions it has attracted. However, the elements of 'shared cultural values and social structures' would seem common to most definitions. Glazer and Moynihan (1975) have summarised the essential characteristics of ethnicity in the following way:

Ethnicity is a new social category . . . [marked by] a pronounced and sudden increase in the tendencies by people in many countries and in many circumstances to insist on the significance of their group distinctiveness and identity and on new rights that derive from this group character.

In the last two decades or so the gradual ethnic awareness among minority groups throughout the world has had a marked impact on education. This ethnic revitalisation movement has asserted itself in most Western countries and in Australia. For example, ethnicity in the United States seemed to emerge from urban deprivation, poverty and other disadvantages experienced by certain groups of society. The electoral successes of Welsh and Scottish nationalists in the 1970s, a surprise to many English people, pointed to a new ethnic political consciousness in Britain.

Along with the rise of ethnicity as a political concept (a concept which has considerable application in the field of ethnic relations) a new wave of educational reformers and researchers has risen in parallel; they have tried to escape from narrow, culture-based research with ethnocentric assumptions. In part this has led to the idea of multicultural, multi-racial and multi-ethnic education (Verma and Bagley, 1979). This is built on the assumption that educational processes should respond to, and respect and foster the ethnic identity of various minority groups in society, as well as making members of the majority group culture aware of the needs and aspirations of minority groups. Although some educationalists and researchers with diverse and often conflicting values, beliefs and assumptions have made proposals to improve the schooling of ethnic minority pupils and to promote equality of educational opportunity, there has been little effort to evaluate their theories and models.

However, this is only one side of the picture. Ethnicity indicates membership of a group which is distinctive in terms of cultural identity, language, religion, physical features perhaps, and life-styles (Bagley and Verma, 1983). The distinctive attribute of an ethnic group is not physical appearance, however, but cultural values. One can argue that it is possible, for example, for social classes to be ethnic groups in a 'racially' homogeneous society if they have distinctive life-styles and values, and if movement between different class groups is restricted. Ethnic groups can be identified not only in terms of cultural values, but through endogamy (finding marriage partners from within one's own ethnic group).

Intermarriage causes a blurring of 'racial' boundaries; often in reaction to these trends dominant racist forces assign individuals arbitrarily to particular 'racial' groups. In the United States, for example, people with more Caucasian than Negro ancestry are nevertheless perceived within the black ethnic group, i.e. defined loosely by their skin colour. Ironically, a person who is black in North

America would be regarded as white in Puerto Rico; in societies like America, being 'black' or 'white' is based on the symbolic definitions of different power structures (Montagu, 1977).

In Britain, for many people, 'ethnicity' implies only physical appearance or skin colour. This view has been a contributory factor in discrimination and prejudice against ethnic minorities from the New Commonwealth. The terms 'Black' and 'Asian' are used to describe people of Caribbean, African and South Asian origin or ancestry. The term 'British' is also used to refer to all people of Britain, regardless of their ethnicity or country of origin. Within this broad framework different ethnic groups are often referred to by national labels: 'English' implies that a person is white with English ancestry; 'West Indian' and 'Asian' are referred to as being within the British group but with a differing kind of ancestry. This situation is further compounded by the indignation of the Welsh, Scots and Northern Irish. They resent being described as English, rightly maintaining their separatist identity.

Racism has also tended to force minority groups to define and emphasise their own ethnicity. This point is illustrated in a study by Jefferey (1976) of 'migrants and refugees'. She cites the experience of Pakistani Christians who migrated to Britain from a preponderantly Muslim country which had not, by and large, respected their Christian identity. They had hoped that because of their Christian identity they would receive more equitable treatment. However, that aspect of their identity was ignored or denigrated. Despite their attempts to assimilate with the Christian culture in Britain, the Pakistani Christians have experienced considerable difficulty and rejection – like other New Commonwealth immigrants – since they have been easy to identify by accent and appearance if not by dress. This type of response clearly indicates that although ethnic minorities are expected to conform to British values, norms and folkways, such conformity does not always bring acceptance. This increasing polarisation of ethnicity in Britain could explain why the results obtained by Robinson (1980) showed that Asian groups with distinctive religious and linguistic identities tend to be highly endogamous.

Smolicz (1980) provides another illustration of how ethnic identity can be imposed. A child, known personally to Smolicz, was born in Australia of British ancestry. When still in his infancy his mother died and he was reared by his uncle's Aboriginal wife (a non-blood relation). In the country town in which he grew up, it was assumed that he must be an Aboriginal. The child told Smolicz how on his way home from school, he was pushed into the creek on a number of occasions by his schoolmates to make him look 'more dirty and brown than he was already'. Smolicz adds: 'In this way he was made to fit in more closely with the "popular" image of the Aboriginal. Following such initiation to the prevailing values, he came to acquire a "part-Aboriginal" identity'.

In Britain, reference is frequently made to 'Asians' and 'West Indians', as ethnic groups. In such references there is an inherent danger of over-simplification since they tend to gloss over the complexities of 'Asian' and 'West Indian' society. Moreover, there is the danger that ethnicity becomes rigidly associated with a particular geographical location, the area of origin of the group. The fact that two people come from the same sub-continent does not necessarily mean they will behave in a more similar manner than two people who do not. Although political and cultural divisions tend to be related, even sub-division into the actual country of origin (for example, sub-dividing 'Asians' into Indians, Bangladeshis, Pakistanis and Sri-Lankans) may hide ethnic and cultural distinctions which ought to form the criteria for group membership.

Identifying the ethnicity of those with immigrant origins is by no means an easy task, nor indeed one which can be achieved without some element of error. Cox (1976), writing about the Australian situation, has highlighted the complex diversity of competing loyalties in ethnic groups, lack of uniform social patterns, their high degree of internal socio-economic stratification, and other factors. Such patterns, according to the author, suggest that there is no unanimity among members of ethnic communities as to whether they wish to retain either their ethnicity or their own culture.

In this research the term 'ethnic group' has been used to mean any group of people with a collected pool of values, customs, behaviours, beliefs and social norms; individuals within that group conform to a proportion of that pool. Such a pool can be referred to as an individual's culture. This operational definition would seem useful for a number of reasons: it allows for considerable variations with any group; it links ethnicity to culture; it avoids confusing ethnicity with geographical origins, language, physical appearance or skin colour. Such factors would, however, usually be linked to the concept of an ethnic group as part of its cultural heritage. It also implies that one individual can be more 'ethnic' than another, in that various individuals draw on their cultural identity to differing degrees when determining their own identity. When using the concept of ethnicity (and, for that matter, that of culture) as a tool to explain differences in behaviour between two or more groups of people, care must be taken not to overstress intercultural differences to the omission of intercultural similarities. In general the differences between ethnic groups are of degree rather than of absolute distinction, with a particular value, attitude or behaviour prevalent in all groups though not with the same frequency. For example, marriage in one form or another is almost universal in the cultural groups, but the processes which lead to the marital bond and the social stigma of breaking that bond differ to a marked degree.

Tajfel (1978) has examined in some depth the forces leading to the strengthening of group identity which results in the overstressing of intercultural differences. He identified three sets of conditions which all lead to 'the appearance of strengthening of "ingroup" affiliations in members of minorities'.

> In the first of these, a common identity is thrust upon a category of people because they are at the receiving end of certain attitudes and treatment from the outside. (Tajfel, 1978)

This sort of process has already been illustrated. Jefferey's (1976) study of Pakistani Christians showed how the reaction of the White community denied them access to the mainstream culture. The case of the boy described by Smolicz (1980) also reflects such external pressures to adopt a particular identity.

> In the second case, a group already exists in the sense of wishing to preserve its separate identity, and is further reinforced by an interaction between the 'inside' and the 'outside' attitudes and patterns of social behaviour. (Tajfel, 1978)

These forces can be seen quite clearly in the issue over separate schools currently under debate. The interaction of white and Pakistani Muslim children within school has been seen by some Muslim parents as a threat to the religious identity of their children. The solution pursued by this group of Muslim parents is to reinforce ethnic identity by strengthening 'ingroup' affiliation by pressing for the creation of separate education systems.

> In the third case, an existing group might wish to dilute in a number of ways its differences and separateness from others; when this is

resisted, new and intense forms of common group identity may be expected to appear. (Tajfel, 1978)

An example of this latter condition may be seen in the development and growth of 'Rastafarianism' in the West Indies and in West Indian communities in Britain and elsewhere. Here, the expression of identity serves to exaggerate the difference between 'Rastas' and others in terms of physical appearance, language, religion, behaviour and so on.

A more recent innovation in analysing the concept of ethnicity is related to cultural pluralism. This model stresses the distinct attributes of ethnic groups and the need for them to live in a sort of separate yet equal harmony. The pluralist approach to ethnicity is based on an appreciation of cultural diversities. The new movement has two broad dimensions:

(a) equality of achievement relating to educational, social and political matters;
(b) retention and maintenance of ethnic identity and distinct culture.

This cultural pluralism is a feature of the 1980s.

Finally, it should be stressed that ethnicity is not an all-or-nothing classification. It is better seen as an amorphous conglomeration of cultural indicators with which the individual identifies. In other words, it is a multi-dimensional concept. In countries such as Australia and Canada, one finds a complex diversity of competing loyalties in ethnic groups, a lack of uniform social patterns and a high degree of internal socio-economic stratification. Such patterns clearly suggest that there is no unanimity among members of ethnic communities as to whether they wish to retain either their ethnicity or their own culture. In a country such as Britain with increasing rates of intermarriage, ethnicity is increasingly defined in political terms, and many pluralistically-oriented Britons have multiple ethnic affinities with white, black and Asian people. Ethnicity is not a permanent feature of one's identity. Ultimately, of course, one might hope for a social system in which all are free to display their own ethnic affinities and to decide the degree of importance they wish to attach to them without jeopardy to themselves or to others.

3 Educational Achievement and Ethnicity

THEORETICAL CONSIDERATIONS

In the research literature the term 'educational achievement' has a range of meanings and applications. Broadly speaking, these could be said to fall within two categories: educational achievement used as an institutional variable and educational achievement used as an individual variable.

The first of these involves an assessment centring on the relative performance of particular schools or other educational institutions, as well as the achievement of different groups in society. In the second the assessment centres on the relative performance of individual pupils or students. In most research such assessment is focused on the performance of groups of individuals, the groups being constructed on the basis of a crude criterion such as ethnicity, social class, and so on.

Within both categories, a variety of factors is likely to mediate on a particular level of achievement. This is because educational achievement is not the product of a single phenomenon (as shown by our study) but represents an interaction between the pupil(s)/ student(s) and the institutional environment. The sort of institutional factors that are typically examined relate to the teachers, the courses, the examinations, teacher–pupil interaction, the school ethos, the peer group and so on.

The studies of Rutter and his colleagues (1979), Taylor (1976), Coleman and his colleagues (1966) and Jencks (1972) provide a useful illustration of these points.

In 'Fifteen Thousand Hours' (Rutter *et al.*, 1979) educational achievement was examined as an institutional variable. Five measures were selected to assess the relative 'success' of the twelve secondary schools in London which took part in the study: the pupils' attendance record, behaviour, examination success, post-school employment and delinquency. The rationale behind the use of such criteria was that the school with the better record on those measures was more likely to be successful in achieving the aims of the school. Contrary to many views, their investigation clearly showed that secondary schools do have an important influence on their pupils' behaviour and achievements. 'The research also showed which school variables were associated with good behaviour and attainment and which were not.' (Rutter *et al.*, 1979).

Taylor's study (1976) 'The Half-way Generation' conducted in Newcastle-upon-Tyne used a different approach. Here educational achievement was assessed in terms of individual performance; the samples being South Asian and their white peers. The criteria selected to assess the relative success of the pupils included: the number and level of public examination passes, length of stay in full-time education and higher education entry. The assumption behind the use of these criteria was that pupils who performed well on them were more likely to be educationally successful than those who did not.

Neither the Rutter study nor that of Taylor was without methodological and technical problems, the principal ones relating to the standardisation of the measurements. Such standardisation is an essential requirement if informed comparisons are to be made, whether between institutions or individuals. Thus Rutter and his colleagues had to find ways of 'controlling' for variations in the quality and intake entering the twelve secondary schools. Taylor was faced with the problem of controlling for variables likely to affect the educational outcomes of individual South Asian and white pupils in Newcastle-upon-Tyne. The strategy that he adopted involved the 'proportional matching' (*see* Verma and Beard, 1981) of his two samples on the basis of school attended, course of study followed and on personal and familial factors. Taylor points out the additional problems such a procedure poses in terms of the significance of his findings: 'This close matching has the advantage of permitting a very precise comparison between the two groups which tries to control for extraneous factors. On the other hand, it means that differences cannot be extrapolated to the populations of Asian and English at large' (Taylor, 1976).

Coleman and his colleagues (1966) also studied educational achievement as an institutional variable. Their study on the equality of educational opportunity conducted in the United States sought to test the hypothesis that the institutional variable would account for differences in achievement among groups of pupils from the dominant and minority cultures. The criteria employed included the age and condition of the school buildings, teaching facilities, class sizes and teacher background. Thus the examination of the institutional variable in their study differs substantially from that used by the Rutter one. The Coleman Report's findings generated controversy, and its critics focused on the statistical analysis employed and the refusal of a large number of cities to participate in the inquiry. Despite these criticisms, Coleman and his associates examined a great number of variables. They found that students' characteristics show stronger association with achievement than do family background or school factors. Studies in Britain (Brimer and Gross, 1977) of public examination successes have shown greater school effects than those evident in the Coleman Report.

Jencks's study (1972) on 'Inequality' should also be mentioned in this context, despite the fact that his work had a broader focus than that in the other studies cited here. His conclusion was that in terms of inequalities present in both British and American society, those inequalities to be found in school and college were insignificant. Such a conclusion, however tenuous it may be considered since it rested on a study of various studies and reports (including the British Plowden Report, 1967) does offer a salutary warning to all who approach the assessment of educational achievement. Whether such an assessment is formulated on the basis of an institutional or an individual variable, the results obtained and the conclusions drawn are to a very large extent dependent upon the criteria employed as the basis of the assessment.

Despite the fact that different criteria have been utilised to assess educational achievement, the results are bound to reflect certain qualities of both the school and the pupil, and to a greater extent the quality of the relationship between the school and its pupils.

EDUCATIONAL ACHIEVEMENT AND RELATED FACTORS

Whether the focus is institution- or individual-oriented, the potential range of criteria available to 'measure' the achievement of pupils/ students is not dissimilar, and relates closely to their performance as 'inmates' of particular institutions or as individuals (usually as members of particular groups).

The most commonly used indicators of public/student achievement are test and/or examination results; at the end of their formal education this yardstick is performance in terminal examinations. In Britain such data are derived typically from CSE, 'O' level and/or 'A' level results. Data thus acquired are irrefutable in the public mind, since examinations have 'official' validation of one sort or another. Moreover particular levels of performance may be a pre-requisite of entry into further or higher education and into various levels of jobs and usually the professions.

Much debate surrounds the extent to which pupils/students are matching up to their 'potential'. This, on the individual level, is associated with whether they are 'achieving' or 'underachieving'. At the institutional level it is concerned with the effectiveness of an institution, usually in comparison with other institutions but sometimes in comparison with national or regional norms; did the particular institution enable its intake of pupils/students to meet their 'potential'?

Once one enters into the field of 'potential' one is on more shadowy ground. Despite the efforts of educationists and psychometricians, no entirely convincing measures of potential have been devised. Typical measures are intelligence tests, which will be considered presently.

Another shadowy area in measurement arises when one is assessing those pupils in a secondary school who take few or no public examinations. In Britain, for example, the 'O' level examinations are targeted at the top 20 per cent of the 16-year-old school population, CSE at the next 40 per cent. Thus there is, theoretically at least, a sizeable proportion of a secondary school whose achievement cannot be effectively measured. In practice, as recent figures suggest, over 90 per cent of the 16-year-old population is entered for at least one subject in public examinations (*The Times*, 7.5.85). Nonetheless there remains a gap where individual achievement is 'not recorded' or where measured achievement at the bottom end has little or no external currency in terms of occupational placement.

Occupational placement is another measure that has been used to assess the achievement of a particular institution or individual. Once again one is entering shadowy ground, since factors relating to occupational placement are not exclusively associated with specific levels of educational achievement. Similarly marginal factors in the assessment of achievement include self-esteem, social class and ethnicity.

Before considering the measures selected for assessing achievement in this study, we will discuss intelligence, occupational placement and self-esteem.

INTELLIGENCE

When considering educational achievement the concept that most readily comes to most people's mind is intelligence. In the popular sense intelligence is a vague but widely used concept: it tends, for example, to be associated with a capacity to do 'well' at examinations being reflected in good examination results. Studies have also suggested that there is a relationship between intelligence tests and public examination results; perhaps because the two types of tests are not dissimilar. Both types of tests require the ability to solve problems within given time limits, assume a certain level of required knowledge and attempt to sample cognitive behaviour at a certain point in time. Thus, it would not be surprising to find that similar factors affect both intelligence test scores and examination results. This does not imply, however, that intelligence (whatever it may mean) determines academic success. It is well established that examination success cannot be adequately explained in terms of measured intelligence.

Within psychology no concept has caused as many problems or encompassed as many misconceptions as has intelligence. Intelligence is a concept employed by psychologists to account for observed variations in performance on certain types of mental tasks. Like heat on gravity in physics it is not something that is directly observable; it can only be inferred from its effects upon particular situations; the usefulness of these theoretical concepts is determined by their capacity to explain observable phenomena.

Intelligence is therefore something that can only be inferred. As a result it has been the subject of much debate, not only in terms of its theoretical components but also in terms of the artefacts devised to 'measure' it. It is fair to say that intelligence is now a discredited term in the field of education unless its usage is carefully qualified. One of the main reasons why it has fallen into disrepute, is its equation with 'IQ'. Despite the well-publicised limitations, scores in IQ tests have long been regarded as a measure of academic potential. The term IQ is seen by many teachers as broadly synonymous with educability. Furthermore, the knowledge of a pupil's IQ score plays a significant part in determining the expectations not only of the teacher but of the education system as a whole about the pupil's potential achievement.

One strand of the intelligence debate has been over the existence of an innate intellectual capacity in the individual, i.e. a genetic endowment. Another has been over the relative contribution to manifest intelligence of any genetic endowment as opposed to that from a particular individual's exposure to particular social factors.

A major criticism of IQ tests is that they are notoriously culture-specific; even the so-called 'culture-free' ones among them have been developed within a particular setting. Thus, whatever their source, IQ tests contain 'loaded' assumptions about intelligence. The suggestion that genetic differences derived from IQ test results among ethnic, cultural and class groups account in large measure for differential school performance is not only of questionable validity; it also tends to divert attention away from more important issues related to the whole educational process.

In addition to the problematic nature of the 'roots' of intelligence, much controversy surrounds the tests devised to 'measure' intelligence and the applications to which these results have been put.

Consider the two following quotations taken from researchers assessing evidence available on intelligence and its measurement:

All the evidence to date suggests the strong and indeed overwhelming importance of genetic factors in producing the great variety of intellectual differences we observe between certain racial groups. (Eysenck, 1971)

An obvious problem for minority children is the content of the test. Items are written by educated, urban, middle-class psychologists and educators to predict the middle-class standards in schools and jobs. While the tests may predict well, they may not be fair examples of intelligence. (Scarr, 1984)

At both a theoretical and practical level, the concept of intelligence has many implications. This is particularly so as far as intelligence tests are concerned for they are often used to assess the relative potential/performance of individuals or groups of individuals. As the quotation from Sandra Scarr shows, there are particular implications as far as ethnic minority children are concerned. The ethnic dimension will be considered more fully in the ethnicity section of this chapter.

What the quotations serve to illustrate here is something of the range of issues generated by the intelligence debate. The immediate concern in this discussion is the contribution of intelligence testing to educational outcomes. The use of tests is still prevalent in Britain and elsewhere. Despite much criticism levelled against them, they continue to be used as a means of classifying school children. On that classification may hinge the range of educational opportunities open to them. Low scores may be a contributory factor in the decision to remove particular children for special schooling, thus removing them from the mainstream of schooling.

In England and Wales group intelligence tests and standardised examinations in English and Arithmetical ability formed the basis of the '11+ examination', used to allocate pupils according to their performance to either a grammar school or a secondary modern. It was based on the naive assumption that there was cultural and social homogeneity in British society. The advent of comprehensive ('all ability') secondary schooling to most Local Education Authorities has virtually brought to an end the use of the 11+ examination. Nonetheless intelligence tests are still administered to children and may play a part in determining their allocation to particular ability bands in their secondary school. There are many LEAs which still use 11+ or similar testing and assessment procedures. A recent survey of LEAs by Gipps, Steadman, Blackstone and Stierer (1983) showed that although between 1972 and 1980 there had been a dramatic decline in standardised testing for selection purposes, there had been an equally dramatic rise in testing for screening, monitoring, assisting transfer and allocating resources. That means, in effect, testing for selection has now become testing to 'aid transfer' within schools. Unfortunately, in some LEAs the two are synonymous. The above authors also comment that:

> We were surprised at the extent to which ability or IQ-type tests of verbal and non-verbal reasoning are still used, since more LEAs test IQ than test Maths. There is certainly a belief among LEAs and teachers that these tests can supply measures of 'potential'.

This sort of allocation by testing will almost invariably condition the range and level of access to public examinations. As with those entering schools, these children once classified (however covertly) tend to conform to the norms and expectations of the group to which they are allocated and those of the teachers taking those classes. Yet on the surface all is respectable: children have been assessed on 'objective criteria' on the basis of performance in tests that often have impressive statistical validity.

OCCUPATIONAL PLACEMENT

Within the British educational system selection criteria used by employers are highly likely to include public examination results in one form or another. Over fifteen years ago Banks (1968) commented that 'one of the main features of a modern industrial society is the extent to which entry to a large range of occupations is increasingly dependent on the acquisition of the necessary educational qualifications'. For some educationists (e.g. Dore, 1976; Collins, 1979; Husen, 1979) such a characteristic is meaningless and damaging, and is described as a social, political and educational disease, while for others educational qualifications are necessary concomitant of a meritocratic society.

Theoretically at least, occupational placement appears to offer a wider view of educational achievement than that obtainable from performance in terminal examinations. Not only can it cater for the most able but also for those whose terminal examinations performance was marginal or non-existent. Certain types of employment (for example, the police force, banking and nursing) particularly in what Cherry (1981) calls the 'instrumental' labour market, and in other post-school avenues in further and higher education, require certain pre-determined minimum levels of examination success as part of their entry criteria.

Public examinations in British schools, as Rutter *et al.* (1979) among others has pointed out, are designed to cater for the most 'able' 60 per cent of sixteen-year-olds. Even if, as we have already noted, perhaps as many as 85–90 per cent of the school population attempts entry in at least one of their school subjects, occupational placement could furnish a more realistic indicator of achievement for school leavers than examination results. Getting a job on leaving school, just as much as gaining entry into some form of further or higher education, would be evidence of achievement and one varying in degree according to the 'status' of the employment obtained and expressed liking for that employment by the individual. Willis (1976) found that certain groups of working class 'lads' did not hold passing examinations as a primary educational objective.

The criterion of occupational placement is not without its limitations. The foremost of these is that employment is not a constant phenomenon; if it were, the chances of obtaining employment commensurate with educational achievement would be identical (or at least similar) from area to area and from year to year. Equally it rests heavily on the assumption that the labour market has a constant capacity to absorb all school-leavers. Although in times of economic stability patterns of employment may be relatively favourable, such a criterion seems inadequate when viewed against the economic and political realities in Britain today. The theoretical and practical problems of the use of occupational placement as a measure of educational achievement can be illustrated by our experiences in this research.

At the theoretical level we could argue that occupational entry represented an interaction between the opportunity structure of the local environment and the abilities of the school-leaver/young worker (Ashworth, 1983) in the same way that examination results represent an interaction between the school and its pupils. Thus it was broadly consistent with our proposed lines of approach. Moreover, since we were dealing with only one area of the country (adjacent cities in West Yorkshire), there was not the same problem of attempting comparisons with economically grossly disparate areas of the country.

However, the economic situation changed markedly in the six years over which this research was carried out. The very high level of unemployment in West Yorkshire, particularly in the youth sector, that began to be felt in the later stages of data collection meant that direct comparisons between individuals from the different phases of this research could not be made on the basis of a measure of occupational achievement, certainly in any quantitative sense. Qualitatively, the occupational entry variable remained a valid indicator, since our analysis rested as much on the perceptions of youngsters as on facts and figures. When we look back on the study from today's vantage point, some two years after the last data on the project were collected, the marked changes in circumstances in terms of employment opportunities between those prevailing in 1977 and those in 1983 are all too apparent.

While there is no denying that over that time the youngsters were becoming increasingly aware of the steep decline in employment opportunities nationally and locally, the full realities of it as far as individual fates were concerned, even as late as 1983, were not fully evident in those perceptions.

SELF-ESTEEM

The literature abounds with a host of terms that theorists have constructed to refer to the concept of 'self'. These include 'self-image', 'self-acceptance', 'self-worth', 'self-evaluation', 'ego-strength' and many others. These terms are used sometimes interchangeably and sometimes to refer to different aspects of personality characteristics and individual functioning in social situations.

The same is also true of the use of 'self-esteem' and 'self-concept' which has dominated the literature. Self-esteem is an affective dimension involving an emotional appraisal of the 'self'; self-concept in its purest sense is a cognitive variable involving the recognition of one's characteristics such as, for example, that one is married, white, tall and male. Self-concept becomes increasingly complex as the child grows older, and is not fully developed until adolescence, when a specific identity begins to emerge. In some recent writings self-concept has been subsumed within the domain of self-esteem.

Life in a multicultural, multi-ethnic society affects not only the attitudes and behaviour of minority group members toward the standards and norms set by the dominant society, but also the responses to themselves and their groups. Thus, an individual's self-perception is a product of his or her contact with others in the wider society. The nature and process of that experience greatly influence the basic ego structure which is the central core of the self. This style of self-perception is succinctly defined by Coopersmith (1967):

> Self-concepts are symbols that blend together the enormous number of varied perceptions, memories and prior experiences that are salient in the personal life of the individual. This concept of one's self . . . is formed by the individual and represents an organisation of separate experiences into some pattern that provides meaning and order in his inner world.

He emphasises that although the terms self-concept and self-esteem are used interchangeably, they refer to markedly different phenomena. According to him:

> Self-concept is the symbol or image which the person has formed out of his personal experiences while self-esteem is the person's evaluation of that image. (Coopersmith, 1975)

Reviewing the literature, Wells and Marwell (1976) suggest that the term 'self-esteem' be used because it is broad enough to provide a common thread that subsumes a diversity of approaches and styles.

Research on the sources of self-esteem has shown the crucial importance of the family in giving the child a secure identity and an adequate self-esteem. Other important sources of self-esteem are the school and peer-group contexts. For example, poor academic performance, being in a low stream, or negative 'labelling' of the pupil can be important sources of poor self-esteem. Supportive peer-groups can, however, counter adverse self-images which schools sometimes transmit – for example to ethnic minority pupils (Bagley, Mallick and Verma, 1979).

'Self-esteem' has been used in the context of both occupational placement and educational achievement. For example, a cardinal tenet of Donald Super's theory (1957; 1981) is that self-esteem is an important determinant of occupational placement. Super has argued that occupational choice represents an expression of the self-concept. The work of Korman (1966; 1970) suggests that a balance exists between an individual's self-esteem and his or her vocational aspirations.

A number of studies have shown that educational achievement and self-esteem are positively related (Labenne and Greene, 1969; Simon and Simon, 1975; Prendergast and Binder, 1975). Those who have poor achievement, relative to their fellows, tend to have poor self-esteem. The relationship between below-average achievement and poor self-esteem appears to hold in a comparative study of adolescents in America and Denmark (Weinland *et al.*, 1976). Nash (1973) has found that poor self-concept is related to a measure of what Bernstein called 'restricted' codes of speech, which account to some extent for the underachievement of children from white, working-class backgrounds. Nash reinterprets Bernstein's theory in median terms, arguing that the self-concept which children acquire is mediated by the linguistic codes of their families. Restricted codes lead to restricted concepts of the self.

Several studies in Britain have also indicated that self-esteem is significantly related to academic achievement for 'disadvantaged' as well as other pupils (Coard, 1971; Milner, 1975). Bagley, Mallick and Verma (1979) found that the most important structural correlations of the 'general-self' component of the Coopersmith Self-Esteem Inventory (Coopersmith, 1967) were being in a low stream at school, being of lower social class and being a 'sociometric isolate'.

Earlier American studies (reviewed by Pettigrew, 1964) tended to suggest that many black children had to a large degree internalised the negative stereotypes which the white majority community held concerning them, and as a result had poorer self-esteem than whites. Some researchers have explained the poor self-esteem of ethnic minority groups on the basis of their ethnic identity and socio-economic status; such evidence has primarily come from the United States where black and white differences are still of paramount importance. It has also been emphasised that ethnicity is a relevant factor in the poor self-esteem which is found in certain cultural and ethnic groups (Ausubel, 1958; Clarke, 1974).

More recent research on children and adolescents in America has challenged this view, however, showing that blacks do not have significantly poorer self-esteem than whites (Coopersmith, 1975; Bagley, Verma, Mallick and Young, 1979). In fact, some studies have even shown significantly better self-esteem in blacks than in whites (Goldman and Mercer, 1976).

Coopersmith (1975), reviewing various studies which have shown a reverse of earlier trends of self-esteem in blacks, concludes that:

> There is increasing evidence that as long as the child stays within an environment in which his culture is in a majority he is able to sustain positive feelings about himself . . .. The social forces that have sought to segregate the Blacks have provided an environment in which these Blacks are insulated against direct assaults upon their feelings. In this environment black children are not teased about their racial characteristics, insulted because of their poor academic performance or demeaned because of the illegitimacy or break-up of their families . . . Insulated by that environment he has the support to reject the low status to which white society assigns his race.

Various explanations have been put forward to account for changed patterns in self-esteem in blacks: there has been a major paradigmatic shift in the way assessment is now carried out and the results interpreted; the effects of the 'black power' movement in America of the 1960s and 1970s might have changed their consciousness (Goldman, 1974); and the effects of changing reference groups in which black children evaluate themselves according to the standards of their black peers, and of black rather than white reference groups (Rosenberg and Simmons, 1972). Other literature, however, suggests that black adolescents in America still suffer from institutional racism in terms of identity formation, and as a result have different conceptions of 'self' from white youngsters.

Studies in Britain of self-esteem amongst ethnic minority children and adolescents have also provided findings which have been both diverse and contradictory. A study by Bagley, Mallick and Verma (1979) revealed that differences in self-esteem between West Indians and whites were confined to boys; West Indian girls were as self-confident as their white counterparts. Similarly, Louden (1978) found that although overall there were no statistically significant differences in self-esteem between ethnic groups, West Indian girls had higher levels of self-esteem than white girls. Louden found that in general, the higher the concentration of the blacks in a school, the higher the levels of self-esteem in the black pupils. The researcher suggested a variety of factors in the school which may influence self-esteem in various ethnic minority groups, including the degree to which minority groups are insulated from various types of white racism.

In the same study Louden (1978) found that pupils of South Asian origin had a higher mean self-esteem score than either West Indian or white adolescents, although this trend did not reach statistical significance. Verma (1981) also obtained small but consistent differences in self-esteem between South Asian and white adolescents, specifically on certain sub-scales of the Coopersmith Self-Esteem Inventory (Coopersmith, 1967). The researcher explained the results of high self-esteem amongst South Asian youngsters as follows:

. . . higher self-esteem in spite of their educational and social disadvantage, is perhaps due to the fact that the adaptation processes of South Asians are mediated through the networks of family and friends, and to some extent through community based self-help systems.

The evidence available so far in this area of research is somewhat inconclusive. This is in part because the attitudes of ethnic minority pupils are likely to have changed over the last decade. Another contributory factor may be imperfections in the instruments used to measure self-esteem, particularly when these are used in cross-cultural settings.

At this point it must be stressed that self-esteem is culturally grounded, and therefore, it is often meaningless as well as invidious to suggest that a particular ethnic group has 'better' or 'worse' self-esteem than any other (Verma, 1984). Self-esteem, as part of an individual's complex identity structure, has different bases and different meanings in different ethnic groups. For example, black identity has special components which reflect the particular experience of being black and surviving in a white-dominated society. In a pluralist framework of society, different ethnic groups have different social-psychological orientations; these differences have to be mutually understood and tolerated if a successful multiculturalism is to emerge (Triandis, 1976).

There is evidence both from theoretical conceptualisation and research findings that schools can play an important part in enhancing the self-concept and self-esteem of all pupils. Pupils from the mainstream culture are in an advantageous position because their norms, life-styles, language, religion and social patterns are reflected both explicitly and implicitly in all aspects of the school system and in society at large. On the other hand ethnic minority pupils suffer from multiple disadvantages both in school and in the wider society. Therefore, comparisons between majority and minority cultures may tend to perpetuate a self-fulfilling prophecy.

For example, ethnic minority pupils in Britain have different identity structures from whites (Coleman *et al.*, 1977). They have a more difficult struggle in educational, social and personal aspects of life than their parents; yet many of them are successful with regard to both achievement and identity development. They can develop positive views of themselves as they grow older. Louden (1978) has argued that with the growth in numbers in minority communities the setting of 'locus of control' changes favourably. In schools where black or Asian groups are in the majority or even a substantial minority, they can more successfully guard against the demeaning slights of racism.

It is clear that studies both in Britain and in the United States have put forward the view that self-esteem is a determinant of educational achievement. The Coleman Report (1966) even concluded that measures of self-esteem were amongst the best predictors of educational achievement.

As pointed out earlier, individual levels of self-esteem are derived from various sources. The contribution of particular sources to the total level of self-esteem varies from individual to individual. Through the analysis of these variations too, self-esteem offers the possibility of additional insights into the processes of achievement.

One of the implicit aims of education is to foster the self-confidence of the pupil. To some degree therefore one might expect to find of that self-confidence reflected in the pupil's self-esteem level and yet not fully reflected in the conventional measure of educational achievement, usually performance in terminal examinations. Thus, particularly among those pupils in Britain either undertaking no public examinations or achieving only marginal success, for example, one or two low grade CSE passes, self-esteem may be able to cast additional light upon them.

The use of self-concept and self-esteem, and the relationship of these two to educational processes are not without their critics. Stone (1981), for example, has provided an extensive critique. Her main thrust is, however, that schools could better concentrate on the imparting of basic skills to their pupils, thus making it possible for them to develop their full potential; if schools concentrated on that fundamental role, then the self-concept and self-esteem needs of pupils would resolve themselves. By seeking to act both as instructors and self-esteem builders, British schools have been all too often unsuccessful on both counts.

That argument centres on *how* schools ought to go about their tasks. Schools whose pupils see themselves as successes or potential successes, whatever the particular levels of individual achievement in public examinations, could be said to be contributing to the overall development of their pupils. Research evidence shows that self-esteem is a crucial concept in understanding personal adaptation in social contexts. Human beings have a powerful need to develop a high level of self-esteem derived from socially approved ways. To this schools can contribute in a positive way, for self-esteem emanates from interactions not only in the home and its immediate surroundings but also in the school and the wider social context.

Quite apart from argument relating to the theory behind any concept, there is also the matter to be considered of the practicability of a particular concept. In the discussion here of self-esteem, consideration must now be given to the ways in which it can be measured.

Three problems beset researchers who attempt to measure aspects of self-esteem in multi-ethnic settings: the problem of selecting an appropriate measure of self-esteem, and establishing the reliability of that measure; the problem of establishing the validity of the measure of self-esteem; and the problem of relating the measure of self-esteem to other theoretical constructs (Bagley, Mallick and Verma, 1979).

Self-esteem, despite imperfections in instrumental terms, nonetheless offers another angle on educational achievement. It may not explain away achievement (or the lack of it) but nor does any other single measure. What it can provide is another dimension of the factors mediating on achievement which, as far as the individual is concerned, tend to rest on cognitive capacities and processes. If no account is taken of the affective components of the psychological make-up of the individual, then the picture that is built up of educational achievement is all the more incomplete.

ETHNICITY

At first ethnicity may not appear to be a relevant dimension in terms of educational achievement. 'Intelligence' examination results, self-esteem and occupational placement have a universal dimension in that they are shown to be associated, in degrees, with individuals. For example, an individual, on the basis of test performance could be deemed to be more able than another. Ethnicity, on the other hand, has no validated scales; no one could be shown to be more 'ethnic' than another.

However, when educational achievement is examined at the societal rather than at an individual level, the ethnic dimension may come into play. In a multi-ethnic society espousing 'equality of outcome', an ethnic analysis of educational achievement offers a useful tool. It may, for example, provide an indicator of the extent to which that equality of outcome is a reality. In more specific terms, it may be able to point to particular factors present in the educational process, that militate against the chances of success for young people from particular ethnic groups. The identification of such factors could then prepare the ground for the seeking of solutions through different educational strategies.

Unfortunately the process of ethnic analysis is not as simple as it might seem. It is compounded by a number of factors, some which are the product of the social sciences which classify (or misclassify) individuals into specific categories or groups of people.

One popularly held view is that differences in the genetic make-up of groups of people are the important determinant of differential educational achievement across ethnic groups. There have been many attempts in the social sciences and other related fields of enquiry to substantiate this view, attempting to add the seal of 'scientific' respectability to folk superstition. Such approaches have been rightly labelled as the 'scourge of scientific racism' (Flynn, 1980).

The work of Jensen (1969; 1973) and Schockley (1972) in the USA and of Eysenck (1971) in the UK would seem to offer highly questionable evidence of the genetic inferiority of peoples from black ethnic groups. Such evidence would, if it were acceptable, absolve the sins of the dominant whites in the face of centuries of their exploitation of the blacks. Given the history of colonialist rampages of white people, it would be comforting indeed for the white power structure if the social sciences could vindicate their actions in the past and enable them to maintain their patronising stance, or outright contempt for those who are considered to be inferior.

In a painstaking analysis of Jensen's findings and of those derived from similar studies, Flynn (1980) rightly bemoans the fact that even in the social sciences, 'the devil as elsewhere appears to have the best tunes'. Flynn (1980), Scarr (1984), and MacIntosh and Mascie-Taylor (1985) among others have all examined the findings of the 'geneticists' and have shown them to be highly suspect. Quite apart from questioning the validity of measures used to assess intelligence, they also attack the way in which the genetic contribution to intelligence is computed.

Recently Mackintosh and Mascie-Taylor (1985) have provided a lucid and cogent exposition of the arguments involved in the IQ debate. They examined studies predominantly from Britain and drew a number of conclusions.

Environmental factors such as 'parental occupation, income, size of family, degree of overcrowding and neighbourhood' are, they found, 'related to IQ among whites'. On the balance of current available evidence, Mackintosh and Mascie-Taylor consider that 'ethnic differences in IQ scores of children from ethnic minorities (in Britain) are probably largely caused by the same factors as are responsible for differences within the white population as a whole'.

Analysing the data from studies on the IQ scores of West Indian children in Britain, they suggest that the scores of even those born in Britain fall 'about 5 to 10 points below the population mean'. However, they argue that when those environmental factors referred to above are taken into account, the difference 'is sharply reduced, in some cases to no more than 3 to 5 points'. They go on to suggest that findings 'tend to argue against those who would seek to provide a predominantly genetic explanation of ethnic differences in IQ'.

As regards the issue of IQ tests themselves, Mackintosh and Mascie-Taylor consider that an unwarranted importance is attached to a child's IQ score. They find no justification for the assumption that an IQ score 'provides a direct measure of [a child's] true worth, or that it predicts his later success in life significantly more accurately than other measures of educational attainment'. They concluded that the

major determinant of inter-ethnic differences in the mean group
intelligence scores was the social environment of the individuals
belonging to those groups.

Flynn (1980) took on Jensen at a statistical level. On the basis of his
calculations he concluded that the maximum variance attributable to
genetic factors would not exceed two fifths. Flynn points out that it is
an interesting question why racists feel a continuing need to 'churn out'
evidence, given the vehemence and irrationality of their case.

Since high correlations have been found between intelligence scores
and examination results, it would seem to be a reasonable assumption
that the latter are just as likely susceptible to differences in the social
environment as the product of any inherent inter-group genetic
differences.

Even if confined purely to socio-economic, cultural and
environmental levels, the analysis of differential educational
achievement across ethnic groups is not without its problems. These
relate both to localised studies as well as to ones dealing with more
than one area. Localised studies may produce findings atypical of the
country as a whole, or produce findings which cannot be generalised
with any confidence. More widely-spread studies would lend
themselves to generalisation, but tend to lack the requisite detail on
the circumstances of the individuals whose performance contributes to
the total 'scores' or means for particular groups or categories of
people.

The data provided by the DES Statistics Branch for the Swann
Committee of Inquiry (HMSO, 1985) are a case in point. The data
were derived from a sample of LEAs (six in 1978/79, five in 1981/82),
not chosen randomly but because those LEAs had 'high levels of
ethnic minority pupils'. That in itself may be regarded as justified, for
there is not an even distribution of ethnic minority groups across
Britain. However, even within those selected LEAs the School
Leavers Survey data could only be provided on ethnic minority groups
in terms of 'West Indians', 'Asians' and 'all other leavers'. Although
the Swann Committee had asked for data on ten different ethnic
catagories for the 1981/82 Survey, those categories would have
produced sub-groups which were too small to give reliable results. In
consequence, such data provided a cruder measure of ethnicity 'than
was ideal'.

This is reflected in the Swann Committee's conclusions on
educational achievement:

West Indian children on average are underachieving at school. Asian children, by contrast, show on average a pattern of achievement which resembles that of white children, though there is some evidence of variation between sub-groups. Bangladeshis in particular are seriously underachieving. Such evidence as there is suggests that of the smaller ethnic minorities, some are underachieving and some are not. Averages, of course, conceal much variation. There are West Indian children who do well, as well as Asian children who are underachieving. (HMSO, 1985, p. 89)

If the role of ethnicity in the process of educational achievement is to be fully understood, there are a number of important considerations.

Firstly, there has to be a sharper definition of ethnic groups than the broad categorisation of West Indian and Asian as reported in the DES School-leavers Surveys and elsewhere. In order to achieve that, better record-keeping would be required at school and Local Education Authority levels. This was a recommendation of the Swann Committee. However, while it may not be a particularly contentious issue in educational circles, the matter of record-keeping, the accuracy of the records and the rights of individual public access to records of whatever description, and the uses to which records are put are not entirely free from controversy. One of the anxieties is that such a strategy of data-collection impinges on individual freedoms. Ethnicity may become an issue of greater individual sensitivity as the proportion of British-born members increases within what are still looked upon as the ethnic minority communities. Indeed, the large group of whites in Britain contains many ethnic minorities – Scots, Welsh, Irish, Northern, Eastern and Southern Europeans, and Travelling People – all assimilated in varying degrees but still in many cases retaining segments of ethnic identity which may influence educational achievement.

Secondly, in terms of being able to generalise upon findings from studies, much will depend on both the scale and the quality of the data. For the time being at least, researchers should focus sharply on many different ethnic groups, and not simply 'West Indians' or 'Asians'. This would enable a clearer picture to be formed of the circumstances of the pupils. Craft and Craft (1983), for example, included social class in their study of educational achievement in a London borough, which threw interesting light not only on the relative advantage of being middle-class in terms of educational outcomes, but also on the underrepresentation of one ethnic minority group within the middle-class category. Unfortunately, that study was only able to provide a broad definition of ethnicity. Furthermore, this was only a localised and small-scale study.

Thirdly, a greater degree of standardisation in data-collection processes in different studies would greatly facilitate inter-study comparisons.

Fourthly and finally, it is important to have proper regard for the uses to which educational research data are put. Current data may well tend to give rise to stereotypes of ethnic minority groups in British schools along the lines that superficially emerge from the Swann Report (1985); thus, West Indian children are 'underachieving', while Asians by and large are doing 'as well as' their white peers. Such stereotypes may have potentially damaging consequences for younger West Indian and Asian children within the British school system. Such a situation, in which the worth of individual school children became conditioned by regular 'league tables' purporting to reflect a rank order of the educationally most adjusted ethnic minority groups would be a travesty of the true educational goal of the development of a plural society, based on equality of achievement and generalised equality of power between all ethnic groups.

4 The Study: Background, Locality and the Schools

In order that this study of educational achievement and ethnicity be understood it is necessary to describe briefly the background and locale in which the research was conducted. Against this backdrop, the schools from which we drew our samples will be characterised.

BACKGROUND

A major feature in British society over the last twenty-five years has been the development of a multi-ethnic community in which people of different and potentially conflicting cultures inhabit the same country, street and classroom. Perhaps the most reassuring aspect of the 'new' society is that it has not been created directly either by war or colonisation.

The history of Britain is marked by many migrations. However, post-war immigration arose largely out of industrial expansion. The economy of Britain like other Western countries expanded at such a fast rate that it had a severe shortage of labour, and people from the New Commonwealth were encouraged to come to Britain to make up the shortfall. Some British employers actively canvassed for workers from overseas, particularly in the colonial and former colonial territories of the Caribbean and of the Indian sub-continent. At that time Britain generally viewed these immigrants as a useful way of meeting the needs of the economic system. Immigrants to Britain from the New Commonwealth, where economic prospects in many parts were poor, felt that migration offered the opportunity of a 'new' life which would mean an improved standard of living and enhanced prospects for their dependents, especially their children. Another category of people coming to Britain on visits, to work or to settle, were Canadians, Australians, New Zealanders and White South Africans as well as Irish people. They represent what is now termed the

Old Commonwealth, that is, the countries which had more or less independent status within the British Empire before World War II.

Coming to Britain, for people from the New Commonwealth in particular, involved very substantial changes in environment – changes in cultural climate and the occupational context of their lives. Adapting to a new culture is not easy for any individual and this often poses problems for immigrants at various levels. Studies have shown that the emigration process, particularly from a developing to a developed country, can form a traumatic experience in the life of an individual. Furthermore, the process requires that the migrants either give up their previous cultural aspects and become part of a new culture, or establish a viable sub-cultural group within the mainstream culture. Either course involves a period of acute insecurity and anxiety, as demonstrated, for example, by Richmond's (1967) study of British and other immigrants to Canada. Thus, the process of settling down in a new cultural environment and establishing satisfactory relationships with one's traditional values, beliefs and attitudes and those prevalent in the host community is extremely difficult.

The different ethnic groups in Britain can be categorised in the following way: Blacks – West Indians and Africans; Asians – Pakistanis, Indians, Sikhs, Bangladeshis, Malaysians and Chinese; Europeans – Italians, Cypriots, Greeks, Poles and Hungarians and so on. Each sub-group relates in different ways to educational, social, occupational and cultural life in British society. However, whenever a reference is made to immigrant groups, the popular assumption is made that the reference is to those people – Blacks and Asians – who have come from the West Indies and the Indian sub-continent respectively. The presence of these groups has generated much discussion about the nature of British society.

Because immigrant groups from the New Commonwealth countries were young, there was a higher proportion of families with younger children among them than in the indigenous population. This has meant a rapid increase in the number of Black and Asian children in British schools. Since the bulk of these immigrants and their families have settled in the major conurbations in London, the Midlands and West Yorkshire, the character of the school population has undergone considerable change. Moreover, given the age structure and cultural patterns of many immigrant groups, the proportion of ethnic minority pupils in schools is likely to rise. Population projections suggest that by 1986, in a total British population of about 54 millions, the population of South Asian origin will number about 1.4 millions; those from the

Caribbean and South America about 1 million; and those from Africa about 150 000. These figures do not differentiate by ethnicity, so the population originating in Africa and Caribbean areas contain a significant minority who are South Asian in origin. In addition, these official figures are biased in the way they treat children of mixed marriages. About 20 per cent of all Blacks and South Asians who are settled in Britain are in mixed marriages with white, European partners (Bagley, 1979). Children of such marriages are counted with the minority 'immigrant' groups.

The highest proportion of migration of South Asian males (mainly from India, Pakistan and what is now Bangladesh), as well as West Indians, took place during the 1960s, other members of their families following shortly afterwards. The largest numbers of South Asian immigrants in Britain have settled in the North West and North East of England, in the Midlands and on the edges of London. Most immigrants from the Punjab and Gujerat are in skilled and commercial jobs, and those from the rest of Pakistan and Bangladesh often work in factories (Deakin, 1970), especially in the textile industry. Recent statistics indicate that there are approximately 1 054 000 people of 'Asian' origin living in Britain or 1.9 per cent of the total population (OPCS, 1983). The comparable figure for those of Caribbean origin living in Britain is 550 000 or 1 per cent of the total population (OPCS, 1983). More than half the West Indians in Britain reside in the Greater London region and the major proportion of the rest live in the Midland cities of Birmingham, Wolverhampton, Manchester, Nottingham and Leicester.

The majority of the early South Asian migrants were young men who had left their families and dependents behind. Their expressed intention was to come to work in Britain for a few years and then to return. However, as time passed the intention to return has been set aside and these people can rightly be regarded as 'settlers' as opposed to 'migrants'. Moreover, their children, born and/or brought up in Britain, are even less likely to return to their parents' country of origin (Anwar, 1979).

To many South Asian immigrants Britain was a foreign land whose language, customs and way of life were profoundly different from their own, and many of the attitudes, values, modes of thinking and behaviour had to be modified in order to adjust to the new society. Such a sudden and massive discontinuity in the way of life of South Asian immigrants posed major problems of general adjustment. Nevertheless, the South Asian community in Britain has been able to maintain a very close contact with traditional kinship networks, and this has played an important role in their adaptation. The adaptation of first-generation immigrants is mediated through a diffuse network of friends, family, and community-based self-help systems, whilst the children of South Asian origin are exposed both to their parents' culture and to those socialisation agencies, particularly school and peer group, which serve the British native white community.

Tinker (1977) has characterised the 'overseas emigrants from India, Pakistan and Bangladesh' as part of *The Banyan Tree*, whose roots travel far underground to form new trees, always connected to the main growth. In this analogy, the South Asian migrants retain strong emotional and cultural ties with the motherland, even several generations after migration.

Brief mention should also be made of the cultural values of the South Asian ethnic groups in Britain. The 'homelands' in the Indian sub-continent lie in a broad area more than two thousand miles across; in this broad area a variety of languages and dialects are spoken, and a number of religious beliefs are practised. Furthermore, rural populations are not in contact with each other and with central authority in the way which developed in the West as a result of industrialisation.

However, there is sufficient contrast between aspects of British culture and aspects of the South Asian cultures and sufficient similarity between these South Asian cultures for some generalisation to have force. Jefferey (1976) states that 'there are several practices in Pakistani Islam which indicate the influence of Hinduism'. She also mentions the contrasts in Muslim and Hindu/Sikh practice, as described in the literature, over the choice of marriage partners, where the former shows a preference for close-kin marriage and the latter prefers exogamous marriage. To exemplify the points Jefferey comments:

> It would be possible to draw up cultural inventories for Punjabi Muslims and Punjabi Sikhs, and establish that . . . there are many similarities. However, . . . the differences in religious allegiance . . . are the crucial element . . . echoed in subtle differences in dress, language . . . and diet.

The above considerations should be kept in mind before making generalisation for the South Asian groups. The South Asian groups which have been involved in the chain migration from the Indian sub-continent over the last thirty years have many common characteristics but there are many differences between them. However, the focus of the most useful and relevant generalisations would seem to be the family structure which must be considered in any understanding of South Asian teenagers and their experiences in British society. It may also be said that the teenager born and brought up in Britain is the product of twentieth-century Western society and does not wholly belong to traditional South Asian societies. The present research throws some light or whether the confrontation between South Asian and Western values in certain matters is a source of difficulty for the South Asian youngsters growing up in Britain.

The West Indians too have their own distinctive cultural, linguistic and social traditions. Jamaicans are the largest group of immigrants in Britain from the Caribbean, forming about 60 per cent of the total. The structure of education and the curriculum of schools in the West Indies has for many decades reflected the British colonial influence.

The West Indians, like the Asians, had to make adjustments to come to terms with life in British society. They have encountered prejudice and discrimination in education, employment and housing. Children of West Indian origin have suffered considerably as a result of a cultural clash between the various West Indian styles and those practised in Britain. Such conflicts are sometimes strongly felt by these children caught between the expectations of the home and those of the school. One of the most important of these is the issue of language.

English spoken with a particular dialect, vocabulary and syntax is the mother tongue of most of the West Indians. Studies have shown that it is the overlapping of elements of patois/dialect and standard English that constitutes the greatest single language problem encountered by West Indian children while learning standard English. However, many teachers and educationists fail to appreciate the cultural significance of Creole, both historically and in contemporary culture. They also fail to understand that Creole is a separate language in its own right (Craig, 1973).

A distinctive feature of West Indians is the strong sense of kinship which extends far beyond the immediate family. It should also be noted that among West Indian parents, particularly working-class parents, there is the widely-held view that education will elevate their children up the social ladder, thus helping them to achieve a better life. Obviously they have great academic apsirations for their children.

In many ways West Indians have been strongly anglicised even before coming to Britain. They were the most assimilationist of all the

New Commonwealth immigrants in the sense that they perceived Britain as their mother country, and, unlike the Asian group, they did not feel that they had to come to terms with an alien culture. In fact, they were least prepared of all the immigrant groups to meet prejudice and hostility in British society. The Jamaican social geographer, Elizabeth Thomas-Hope (1982) compared the adjustment to migration, and satisfaction with achieving goals of migration, of similar groups of Caribbean migrants to the UK, Canada and the United States. She interviewed several hundred Caribbean respondents in London and other centres in the UK, in New York, Hartford and Boston in the US, and in Toronto and Hamilton in Canada. The highest levels of satisfaction with achieving the goals of migration were those reported by West Indians in the US centres, closely followed by those in Canada; but levels of satisfaction were dramatically lower in respondents from the UK.

RESEARCH LOCALITY

We now turn to the West Yorkshire cities of Leeds and Bradford (location of this research) which have had a long history of acting as hosts to immigrants. The two areas not only differed from each other in their demographic characteristics but, as we will see shortly, contained a heterogeneity of neighbours within themselves. Table 4.1, derived from the OPCS 1981 Census (HMSO, 1983) provides an indication of the relative size of the New Commonwealth and Pakistani population, as categorised by the birthplace of the head of household, living in the whole West Yorkshire area as well as that of those living in Bradford

TABLE 4.1   *Percentage of New Commonwealth and Pakistani persons usually resident in private households*

	Total	New Commonwealth and Pakistan* (NCWP)	NCWP residents as percentage of total
West Yorks	2 000 305	118 372	5.9
Bradford	449 897	50 442	11.2
Leeds	688 561	27 807	4.0

* category determined by birthplace of head of household
SOURCE   OPCS 1981 Census.

TABLE 4.2 *Percentage of New Commonwealth and Pakistani children aged 5–15 normally resident in private households*

	Total	New Commonwealth and Pakistan*	NCWP children as percentage of total
West Yorks	341 933	32 241	9.4
Bradford	78 044	14 105	18.1
Leeds	113 481	6 888	6.1

* category determined by birthplace of head of household
SOURCE   as Table 4.1.

TABLE 4.3 *'Ethnic'* breakdown of New Commonwealth and Pakistani children aged 5–15*

	NCWP (total)	East Africa as %	Caribbean as %	India as %	Bangladesh as %	Other NEW as %	Pakistan as %
West Yorks	32 241	2.2	15.8	30.0	2.5	4.5	44.7
Bradford	14 105	2.1	7.1	24.0	3.4	2.4	61.0
Leeds	6 888	4.0	32.0	30.1	3.2	8.2	22.1

* as categorised by birthplace of head of household
SOURCE   as Table 4.1.

and Leeds. Table 4.2 provides a similar picture for children aged between 5 and 15 years, while Table 4.3 provides the breakdown proportions of the different sub-groups within the total New Commonwealth and Pakistani child population.

In Bradford in the nineteenth century, a German quarter was established and part of the city centre is still referred to as 'little Germany'. The roads and houses which maintained Bradford's economic momentum in the course of its development as a textile centre were built by Irish labour. There was also a tendency for Eastern European immigrants, particularly Poles, to settle in specific areas of Bradford (for example, Little Horton and Great Horton) but no specifically Polish areas exist now; in moving out from the terraced property which they originally occupied near the city centre, many East Europeans have now scattered into semi-detached properties on the city outskirts. With one marriage partner English, and the other usually English-speaking and white, this has meant easy family assimilation into the host society. However, a Polish-Catholic church, Polish clubs, shops selling foods preferred by the Polish community, and Saturday morning language schools (in Polish, Ukrainian, Latvian and Lithuanian) are ample evidence that the East European community has not abandoned aspects of its cultural background, although it is now an integral part of the community. East European 'voluntary' workers, therefore, filled the gap left by the labour shortage of the post-war years until the arrival of the first immigrants from the Indian sub-continent. It is interesting to note that, in 1934, J. B. Priestley expressed somewhat premature regret that Bradford would never again enjoy the diversity of cultures which he himself met on returning to the city (Priestley, 1934).

The first South Asian immigrants in Bradford arrived mainly from the Mirpur district of Azad Kashmir (Free Kashmir), and from both sides of the Punjab border; a small proportion came from Sylhet, in what is now Bangladesh. Chain migration was aided by heavy recruitment by two major sectors of industry – transport and textiles. It was in these industries that the very early New Commonwealth immigrants were employed in the 1950s. Initially employed in textiles as a replacement for white workers who had gone elsewhere in search of higher wages, the immigrant workforce enabled industry to enter a period of heavy investment by providing labour prepared to work unsocial hours, and maximised the productivity of new machinery.

The 1981 Census also shows that 6.5 per cent of Bradford's population consists of 'first generation' migrants from the New Commonwealth and Pakistan. This compares with the figures provided earlier in Table 4.1 showing that the NCWP population of Bradford is 11.2 per cent of the total. Table 4.4 shows that this discrepancy is partly accounted for by the fact that nearly 80 per cent of

TABLE 4.4   *Ethnic Breakdown of Bradford children aged 5–15*

		Totals	Percentage of all children	Percentage of NCWP children	Percentage UK born
All children		78 044			
NCWP children		14 105	18.1		78.0
ethnic divisions of NCWP total	East African	290	0.4	2.1	64.5
	Caribbean	1 005	1.3	7.1	98.0
	Indian	3 422	4.4	24.0	87.0
	Bangladeshi	481	0.6	3.4	39.1
	Pakistani	8 573	11.0	61.0	68.3
	Other NCW	334	0.4	2.4	83.0

the children in those households were born in the UK. (Of children under 5 the 1981 Census shows that 90 per cent were born in the UK.)

What should be noted, however, is that the process of settlement is not uniform among the various segments of the NCWP population. Only 4 in 10 children in Bangladeshi households in Bradford were born in the UK compared with a figure of 8 in 10 for NCWP households as a whole. It should also be noted that children in Caribbean households in Bradford were virtually all born in the UK. In reality very few South Asian and West Indian children in British schools in the 1980s were born outside Britain.

With the exception of two comprehensive schools which were purpose-built in the early 1960s, the secondary schools in Bradford became comprehensive in 1967, whilst retaining older premises. Where new premises have been subsequently built, prior to the freeze on capital expenditure, they were located predominantly in the outer areas of the city. This has often resulted in lengthy bus journeys from the inner city for many pupils. Due to the distribution of immigrant settlement in Bradford (the central areas containing by far and away the greater proportion of the ethnic minority communities), the long bus journeys fall disproportionately upon these youngsters. The existence of comprehensive schools in Bradford does not imply a wholesale move towards mixed ability teaching; streaming in one form or another occurred in all the schools involved in the present study. Bradford schools are divided into a tripartite system of first, middle and upper schools, though a number of local teachers have reservations about this model.

The City of Bradford Metropolitan District, a County Borough prior to local government reorganisation in 1974, maintains a sizeable battery of statistics relating to aspects of the Metropolitan District's life, including housing, employment and education. The Council publishes these regularly in publications such as *District Trends* (BMDC, 1984) and, published after that, in *Bradford in Figures* (BMDC, 1984). These statistics are built up from a variety of sources including governmental ones such as the OPCS Census and from its own monitoring exercises.

Amongst other things, these statistics trace the growth and the projected growth of the ethnic minority population and of its children in particular. Current indicators are that by 1991 one third of the school population will come from the ethnic minority communities.

They also shed light on the linguistic diversity within Bradford's ethnic minority communities and specifically in the Authority's schools. A survey conducted by the Directorate of Educational Services in March 1981 (see for example, *Bradford in Figures*, BMDC, 1984) showed that 17.5 per cent of the Authority's school population used a language other than English. The proportion in first schools (18.6 per cent) was slightly higher than that in the middle and upper schools (14.3 per cent).

In 1977 approximately 31 per cent of the total South Asian school population faced severe language problems. Although the proportion among those in the upper school age range (about 12 per cent) was much lower it is beyond doubt that language problems will have mediated upon the situation of young people taking part in the first phase of this research.

An elaborate system of support for non-fluent English speakers has been worked out over the years during which Bradford has had significant numbers of such youngsters. Even in 1981, just over 1 in 10 of youngsters of school age using a language other than English were in language centres. These prepared children for transfer to schools as soon as they were considered capable of coping with the school curriculum. They offered children crash courses in English as a Second Language (E2L) and general preparation for education in Bradford's schools.

While the E2L service in Bradford has rapidly developed a system of language support both in the language centres and extensively in the mainstream schools, there were many lessons to be learned, particularly in the early days of the service.

Some criticisms were made by E2L teachers to the researchers during the first stage of this research regarding the E2L provision in schools. Selection procedures for E2L staff were seen as suspect by some teachers and it was felt that these teachers were not invariably utilised to the best advantage of ethnic minority pupils. Many schools used to operate a 'block withdrawal' scheme of teaching which tended to segregate and label *all* 'Asian' pupils. While no hard evidence existed to suggest either beneficial or detrimental effects as a result of dispersal, it was undoubtedly considered an offensive policy by many prominent members of the Asian community.

Leeds is the traditional capital of West Yorkshire, although the regional administration centre since before 1974 has been Wakefield. A larger city than Bradford, Leeds has a population approaching 700 000. Its industrial structure diversified at a far earlier stage and

hence the decline of textiles led to a less acute problem than
Bradford's.

Leeds, like Bradford, has a considerable history of immigration.
Among the earliest immigrants were the Irish and the Jews. As Table
4.1 shows, the New Commonwealth and Pakistan population of Leeds
is smaller in size than that of Bradford, making up some 4 per cent of
the Leeds population. The NCWP school population is 6.1 per cent.
As in Bradford, the vast majority (83 per cent) of NCWP children are
UK born, as is seen in Table 4.5. The table shows that the pattern of
settlement of the various sub-groups is not uniform; once again the

TABLE 4.5 *Percentage breakdown of Leeds children*

All children aged 5–15	NCWP	EA	C	I	B	P	Other NCW
113 481	6 888	276	2 193	2 109	222	1 524	564
As % of all Leeds children aged 5–15	6.1	0.2	1.9	1.9	0.2	1.3	0.5
% UK born	83.3	63.4	98.4	87.0	34.2	68.4	80.3
As % of NCWP Leeds children aged 5–15		4.0	32.0	30.1	3.2	22.1	8.2

NCWP New Commonwealth and Pakistan
EA   East African
C   Caribbean
I   Indian
B   Bangladeshi
P   Pakistani

proportion of UK born Bangladeshi children (34.2 per cent) is well
below that of all NCWP children, against 98.4 per cent of those from
Caribbean households.

Apart from the difference in scale of the NCWP populations of
Leeds and Bradford, there is another important difference. In Leeds
people from Caribbean and Indian households make up about 30 per
cent each (29.5 per cent and 31.1 per cent respectively) of the total
NCWP population; those from Pakistani households make up just
under one fifth (19 per cent) and those from 'other' New
Commonwealth households about one eighth (11.9 per cent). Fifty-
eight per cent of Bradford's NCWP population come from Pakistani
households and almost a quarter (24.6 per cent) from Indian ones;

those from Caribbean households are only 7.3 per cent of Bradford's NCWP population. People from Bangladeshi households are about 3.5 per cent of the NCWP in Bradford and Leeds (3.6 per cent and 3.3 per cent respectively). Those from East African households, for the large part East African Asians, make up 2.9 per cent of Bradford's NCWP population against 5.3 per cent of that of Leeds.

As the above figures show, the NCWP population of Leeds is very different in composition; in Bradford the best known 'immigrant' area is the Manningham ward with its settlement of Pakistanis and Bangladeshis. The corresponding area in Leeds is Chapeltown; there the population is predominantly West Indian in origin. In Leeds the South Asian population is comparatively small, consisting mainly of Punjabis, Sikhs and Bangladeshis, although Leeds has attracted larger numbers of East African Asians. Perhaps the most significant difference between Leeds and Bradford is in the level of self-consciousness regarding the immigrant population. Leeds is well known for its football team, as the centre of Yorkshire cricket (though Bradford does have a county cricket ground) and as a diverse industrial and commercial centre. Bradford, once famous as a wool centre, is now most commonly associated with 'immigrants'. As was seen earlier, much statistical work is undertaken by the local authority to monitor its NCWP population; in Leeds, few statistics regarding, say, education are readily available. Moreover, where concern does exist it tends to concentrate on the behavioural problems of children of West Indian origin.

Because of reorganisation (in 1974) in which the Leeds City Council Education Committee became responsible for some schools which had previously come under the former West Riding County Council Education Committee, three types of schooling system exist within the area. The dominant system is the 'lower', 'middle' and 'upper' type in which the pupils change schools at ages 9 and 13 years. The areas covered by the old West Riding Authority operate a two-tier system of 'primary' and 'secondary' in which the children change schools at 11 years. The third system is used uniquely in the Otley district and consists of a three-tier system in which the children change schools at 8 and 12 years.

Although, as was stated earlier, Leeds has a history of migrant labour, the ethnic origins of the pupils within the education authority were not recorded. It was thus difficult to make any accurate assessment of the total number of ethnic minority children receiving their education in the authority. The exception to this concerns those pupils who attended one or other of the two Jewish schools (one primary and one middle). These pupils accounted for some 450 pupils or approximately 0.5 per cent of the total school population of Leeds (105 000).

An Immigrant Reception Centre was provided for children who had not previously attended school in Britain and who it was felt would profit from a period of adjustment to the new environment. This centre was used for assessment in which any particular educational needs could be identified, including training in English as a second language. Although the centre was also seen as a place where the medical authorities could conduct such checks as they felt appropriate, the authority took care to indicate that this was not a major purpose of the centre.

In addition to the reception centre the authority employed a language development team which consisted of a number of peripatetic teachers who were deployed in schools where there were a considerable number of children who had little or no English. They were concentrated mainly in primary schools and, in particular, worked with the five to seven age range. However, some of their work was conducted with the middle schools. The needs of the various schools were assessed on a termly basis and the members of the team were allocated accordingly.

Decisions about whether a particular child was appropriate for the Immigrant Reception Centre were made by the Headteacher of the school concerned in consultation with the Allocations Section of the Education Department. The Authority also pointed out that children returning to Leeds after periods spent abroad could be re-admitted to their schools without further formality.

It can be seen from this résumé that policy concerning ethnic minority pupils in Leeds was much less formalised than that within Bradford. Whether this was a good or a bad stance depends very much on the stress one places on E2L teaching and cultural integration. Nevertheless, one suspects that because the actual number of pupils with recognisable language difficulties was much smaller than in Bradford (the major group of immigrants in Leeds being of West Indian origin), the perceived need for a highly organised system of initial training was less. These structural differences would support Little's contention (1978) that the obvious language difficulties of South Asian youngsters have resulted in their receiving more attention than West Indians whose first language was non-standard English (see also DES, 1985).

South Asians and West Indians both in Bradford and Leeds are disproportionately over-represented among the most vulnerable groups in the working population: the young, unskilled and semi-skilled manual workers, and those working in declining industries. National statistics show that between February 1980 and February 1981 – more or less the mid-point of our longitudinal study – ethnic minority unemployment rose by 83 per cent compared with a rise of 66 per cent in overall unemployment. The figures for unemployment in Bradford and Leeds over the period in which our investigations were conducted are shown in Table 4.6.

TABLE 4.6 *Unemployment and vacancy figures: Bradford and Leeds*

All workers		June 1979	June 1980	Sept 1981	June 1982	Sept 1982
Leeds	Unemployed	8 174	10 308	16 842	17 662	39 712
	Vacancies	1 851	1 187	641	713	1 623
	Difference	6 323	9 121	16 201	16 949	35 089
Bradford	Unemployed	8 117	10 430	17 927	18 367	23 061
	Vacancies	1 033	618	399	537	751
	Difference	7 084	9 812	17 528	17 794	22 310
Immigrants		June 1979	June 1980	Aug 1981	June 1982	
Leeds	South Asian	236	215	895	1 250	
	West Indian	223	202	217	375	
Bradford	South Asian	1 155	2 590	3 185	3 833	
	West Indian	360	377	447	464	

SOURCE Manpower Intelligence Unit, Leeds

Within the sphere of youth employment, the pattern is even worse. This is dramatically illustrated by the following quotation taken from 'District Trends 1984' (BMDC, 1984):

In 1979 just under half of Bradford's black school leavers seeking work had found jobs by September compared to seven eighths of white school leavers. By 1983 the situation for both groups was worse. But while 37% of white school leavers still managed to find jobs by September, the proportion of successful black school leavers had fallen to just 7% – 1 in 14.

The results of an attitude survey conducted by the Commission for Racial Equality (CRE, 1981), serve to highlight this issue. They found that nationally 88 per cent of West Indians and 80 per cent of 'Asians' agreed with the sentiment that at times of high unemployment ethnic minorities tend to suffer most. Again, some 86 per cent of West Indians and 78 per cent of 'Asians' agreed that it was more difficult for ethnic minority people to get jobs than it was for whites. They also found that 83 per cent of West Indians and 58 per cent of 'Asians' believed that their status in British society was inferior to that of white people. The authors concluded that:

A general sense of material deprivation is a breeding ground for frustration and unrest, and a particularly worrying feature of the survey findings is the pronounced perception of deteriorating race relations amongst British educated young people in the ethnic minorities. (p. 17)

This has been a general pattern for many immigrant groups: whatever their initial attitude to British culture, the British attitude has generally been one of aloofness and non-acceptance. The reaction on the part of the ethnic minority communities has been to withdraw as far as possible into their own networks and resources, and indeed to re-establish religious and cultural traditions which were lapsing.

In examining attitudes of the native population to South Asian or West Indian ethnic minority groups it is not suggested that every white Briton is racist. Research (Bagley and Verma, 1979) has shown that over 20 per cent of the population advocate the idea of cultural pluralism and its counterpart of multi-cultural education. Unfortunately, as Parekh (1978) comments, 'The sections of public opinion that have hitherto had the greatest impact have been racist. They have dictated the terms of the public debate and the basic outlines of the government policies. The non-racist sections have been able to do little more than moderate the tide of racism and, on occasion to extract a few concessions.' (p. 48) Whatever the explanation, the fact remains that the New Commonwealth immigrants have been subject to varying degrees of prejudice and discrimination and that after thirty years or so of having black and brown ethnic minority groups living in this country the educational system has not fully come to terms with the fact that Britain has become a multi-ethnic, multicultural society.

THE SCHOOLS

The first two phases of the study drew their samples from seven schools in the Leeds and Bradford area of West Yorkshire. These schools are denoted by the letters A to G. Two further Bradford schools (H and I) provided the sample for the third phase. In all, nine schools were involved in the study.

In the first phase our aim was to seek schools of differing environments and sizes and with varying porportions of ethnic minority pupils. In Bradford, a choice of five schools from twelve was offered, and in Leeds the two schools were selected by the LEA. The main impact of this was that the schools lacked the degree of variation which had been hoped for, particularly in Leeds where the two schools were remarkably similar.

In phase two, a follow-up phase, pupils and ex-pupils from the same seven schools were involved. In phase three, however, Bradford allowed a free choice of schools. Two schools were approached that had not been included in the previous sample. Here two schools were sought that were as similar as possible in catchment area, record of educational achievement (in terms of public examination results) and proportion of ethnic minority pupils, but as dissimilar as possible in organisation, ethos, formality and other aspects.

It should be remembered that the following descriptions of the schools refer specifically to the period of research. Some of the schools' ethos, organisation and staff might have changed and our findings do not necessarily apply to the particular schools as they are today. Nevertheless, there is every reason to believe that the results obtained and the conclusions we have drawn are still applicable to schools as a whole.

School A

Located in an outlying area of Bradford, near a large council estate created by early 1960s slum clearance, school A was an ex-secondary modern mixed comprehensive. The school had approximately 1200 pupils of whom 10 per cent were of 'New Commonwealth' origin, mainly from the Indian sub-continent. The proportion of West Indian children was very small. The E2L department was run by an energetic young teacher who had, single-handed, abolished the old system of block teaching of 'immigrant' children and instituted a system of withdrawal, though this did *not* apply to fifth formers we studied who were still taught as a group. The operation of a withdrawal system seemed likely, however, to affect the careers education of ethnic minority pupils, since those lessons were perhaps the most likely to be chosen as suitable for the withdrawal of individuals.

Discipline in the school was based on an extremely traditional approach, with corporal punishment being administered by the Deputy Headmaster. Though the Head's approval was sought for participating in the research project, he had no comments to make on the subject and the strategy of the research. He appeared fundamentally uninterested, and passed the responsibility over to the E2L teacher.

Careers education was managed by a middle-aged woman, who tended to hold stereotyped and disillusioned views of contemporary youth which she did not hesitate to reveal in the classroom, much to the annoyance of some pupils. There were no ethnic minority teachers on the staff.

School B

One of the two original purpose-built comprehensives in Bradford, which has been under the same headmaster since 1962, this school was very traditional in its standards. The staff wore gowns, and the general appearance was seen as vital in maintaining morale. The headmaster's professed interest in the notion of a 'benevolent dictator' to rule the country undoubtedly had some relevance to the way the school was run. There were two ethnic minority teachers at the school, but to some of the staff, they were considered as something of a 'problem' from the point of view of stresses arising both in the classroom and the staff-room.

There was no formal careers education as such. The school counsellor included careers work in his pastoral work, but strictly on a 'come and get it if you are interested' basis. He felt that this encouraged individual initiative, though he was not forthcoming as to the fate of individual pupils lacking in initiative.

Approximately 1300 children attended the school, which was situated five miles outside the city centre. Some 13 per cent of the pupils were from a New Commonwealth background, roughly a quarter of them being of West Indian origin.

School C

Located in a village six miles from the centre of Bradford, this school was an ex-grammar school, turned comprehensive in 1967. As the Headmaster admitted, it was probably more middle-class than many other schools in Bradford, due to its catchment area. This had some beneficial effects on behaviour as, for example, truancy was well below the rate for most of the other schools involved in the study.

The Headmaster, who had been in the post two years but was previously Assistant Headmaster, had in the past occupied the post of Careers Master in another school, and as a result assigned a high priority to careers education which started in the fourth year, and was to be extended into the fifth year, if resources allowed. The Head of the Fifth Year also was highly conscious of careers problems, since he had to cope with many of the pupils' most pressing questions.

This school was comparatively small, with only about 800 pupils with a seven-form intake. Ten per cent or so of the school population had origins in the Indian sub-continent, 2 per cent were of West Indian descent. Most pupils came from an inner city area on the radial road which runs through the village. This inner city area varies between one of the worst slum areas of Bradford, and a neighbouring area with a predominantly middle-class, professional component in the population. Therefore, the ethnic minority children in the school came from varied backgrounds.

School D

One of the most modern purpose-built comprehensives in Bradford, this school had been formed three years previously from two single-sex schools and occupied a site overlooking the city centre. The facilities were very extensive and furnishings all combined to give an air of opulence.

The school was divided into faculties: languages, science, humanities and crafts, which were located in different areas of the school. There was a fully-equipped language laboratory, a computer terminal, a university-sized lecture theatre, and a drama studio (used, to the Deputy Head's distaste, as a discothèque by a local youth club). The school operated a banding system and within its academic, low academic and non-examination bands the pupils were streamed. Whilst, ostensibly at least there was concern to provide every pupil with a *suitable* education, the Head was keen on maintaining 'academic standards'. The Careers Master felt that this had had a deleterious effect on careers education, which had been the first section of the school's activities to be curtailed when educational cut-backs affected the school.

Approximately 1400 children attended the school at the time of the study, of whom 15 per cent came from the New Commonwealth, predominantly the Barkerend area of the city where the majority of the city's Indian Punjabis live. Only 2 per cent of the school population were of West Indian origin.

School E

Located on two sites, some quarter of a mile away from each other (which frequently caused problems in class attendance) this school had a number of distinctive features. It was a community school, involving itself in a number of outside activities such as old peoples' luncheon clubs. It was the only school in the LEA which accepted physically handicapped children in the classroom. It was also the only school which had abolished corporal punishment, and this led to its 'rough' reputation which still existed at the time of the research. Its catchment area included some of the large post-war council estates in Bradford, and this had added to its.reputation. One of the most striking elements, particularly to a research worker trying to make arrangements for the administration of a questionnaire, was the diffusion of power. Rather than a rigid hierarchical structure, with the Head at the top, authority and responsibility were delegated downwards as far as possible. As a result the school frequently appeared disorganised though the informal atmosphere was appreciated by pupils. Non-attendance was very high. The school had 1300 pupils, of whom approximately 17 per cent were from the New Commonwealth (South Asian 13 per cent, West Indian 4 per cent).

School F

Located on the ring road to the west of the city, this school was an amalgamation of two single-sex grammar schools which had a city-wide catchment area. Many staff were still imbued with the grammar school ethos, and viewed comprehensive education with a degree of anxiety. Whilst most subjects had been banded, and internally streamed within the bands, some humanities subjects, grouped together under the title of 'community studies' had been taught on a mixed ability basis. This experiment had not been viewed as a success, and all classes were returning to a streaming system in 1979. This school was the only one in the study to be organised on a 'house' basis, and a good deal of importance was attached to this form of supervision and pastoral care. This included careers education. Though the Head Teacher was previously a careers master he did not see formal careers lessons as playing an important role, placing more emphasis on individual interviews with the five teachers allotted to careers counselling in the houses and the sixth form, and on the links which had been built up with local colleges and industries.

The South Asian population of the school was approximately 10 per cent, and the West Indian 2 per cent at that time.

School G

Located near the ring road on the east side of the city, this school was again an amalgam of two single-sex grammar schools, turned comprehensive two years previously, though in this instance the sites were farther apart. The senior staff had been in their respective posts for over eleven years and as a result, the school had even more of an attachment to the grammar school ethos. The Head and Deputy Head gave the impression of struggling to swim against the tide. Careers were formally taught, by a comparatively young and enthusiastic man, who appeared very conscious of the existence of discrimination against ethnic minority youngsters, not merely at the employment level, but also in further education.

Again, the proportion of South Asian pupils was around 10 per cent, and that of the West Indian 2 per cent.

School H

Located some 1½ miles outside the centre of Bradford, this school drew its pupils primarily from a large council estate and several smaller private housing areas. The school was noticeably overcrowded because it had some 500 more pupils than it had been designed for, which was 800. Nevertheless, this does not imply that the school was chaotic; the organisation of the school was such that each pupil was aware of where he/she had to be and how to get there. Outwardly this was an informal, non-uniformed school which appeared to stress personal worth to a greater extent than academic excellence. However, the performance of the pupils in years previous to that during which the research was undertaken was on a par with the best in the area. The Headteacher himself took responsibility for careers education, pending the appointment of a specialist careers master. The researchers were impressed by the ease at which the data-collection was conducted within the school, and the understanding of the Headmaster of topics relating to ethnically plural schools. The proportion of ethnic minority pupils was approximately 25 per cent (South Asian 23 per cent and West Indian 2 per cent).

School I

Located some 3 miles outside the city centre (Bradford), this school had excellent facilities in terms of accommodation; for example, a swimming pool was available on site. Although outwardly the school appeared well organised, research was difficult to conduct, not least because insufficient preparations had been made for each of the researchers' visits. The school was formal in terms of approaches towards education and the upholding of traditional values of academic excellence. The pupils wore school uniform and a special unit had been established for 'gifted children'. Although the proportion of ethnic minority pupils was about 20 per cent (South Asian 17 per cent, West Indian 3 per cent), no special provisions were in operation, the Headteacher being proud of the 'we treat every child alike' policy within the school. The catchment area of the school included a large council estate and a variety of private housing.

THE SAMPLES

In the first phase of the research, over a thousand pupils were drawn from the 1977–78 fourth forms of seven schools. All pupils completed the Vocational Adaptation Questionnaire. For the purposes of detailed analysis the questionnaires of 220 ethnic minority youngsters were extracted along with a matching sample of 220 white youngsters. These sub-samples were matched on sex, school and to reflect as far as possible the ability range. The administration of the questionnaire was conducted during school time.

A year later when pupils were in their fifth year, a further sub-sample of 200 pupils was derived substantially from the previous sub-samples of ethnic minority and white youngsters. This new sub-sample (i.e. 200) was, however, skewed towards ethnic minority youngsters who made up 75 per cent of it. They were subjected to a battery of tests as well as being interviewed. During this period interviews were also conducted with parents, members of the community, teachers and careers officers. In phase two which was a follow-up, our aim was to re-examine that final sub-sample from phase one. By then the majority had left school.

In phase three a fresh sample was sought, this time from schools H and I. It consisted of the whole 1982/83 fifth year groups of the two schools and numbered 413 youngsters of various ethnic groups. A questionnaire was administered to them in mixed ability classes. In addition an interview sample of 82 youngsters was sought. This comprised 38 sixth formers from the two schools and 44 youngsters who had left those schools at the end of the 1981/82 school year. A letter of introduction was sent by the headteacher of the schools to each of the young people, telling them of the purpose of the research. This was followed up by telephone contact or personal call by the researchers. A response rate of 90 per cent was achieved.

5 Context of the Research and Early Findings

THE GENERAL CONTEXT

In addition to educational issues outlined earlier, questions about the ethnocentric stance of testing and selection procedures, of the school curriculum and of teaching styles have steadily come to the fore in the last two decades. The process has been accelerated by the increasing proportion of ethnic minority schoolchildren born not across the waters but born in the same street or the same hospital as their white peers.

Another contributory factor has been the proportion of ethnic minority youngsters reaching school-leaving age and faced with the reality of the world of work. In a shrinking youth employment market that reality has been soured, and has pointed to how ill-equipped many of them are to advance personal aspiration and family fortune. Some of that attendant frustration found its expression in the disturbances of Brixton, Toxteth and Bristol during the summer of 1981, and more recently in Birmingham in October 1985.

The brunt of unemployment has borne particularly heavily on ethnic minorities (Smith, 1981), and unemployment amongst ethnic minority youth is four times the level in young whites (CRE, 1980; Runnymede Trust, 1981). Unemployment among minority groups is more sensitive to general economic changes, and its level rises or falls more steeply than employment among ethnic majority groups. Unemployment among West Indian males and Asian females is especially volatile (HMSO, 1981). Widespread unrest among unemployed young people in many British cities was hardly surprising in these circumstances. In Liverpool where the 1981 disturbance was most desperate, many of the young people involved were neither black nor white, but were descendants of a century of ethnic mixing – English, West African, Irish, West Indian and Chinese (Waller, 1981).

Unless these young people can be given a genuine chance of social mobility, we may not have seen the last of the dramatic social unrest.

In an editorial on the urban disturbances of summer 1981, *The Times* commented obliquely on the combinations of racial harmony and economic deprivation which the population of Liverpool presents:

> Britain is a multiracial society with a good deal of racial hatred, yet little is done to enable people to comprehend and combat the evil of racialism. It will not be resisted by preaching integration. That is the fallacy of the sixties. It is unrealisable, it is questionable if it is desirable, and it raises more fear and animosity than it dissipates with its overtones of inter-racial sex, marriage and a coffee-coloured Britain. (*The Times*, 7 July 1981, p. 13)

The Fifth Report from the Home Affairs Committee, 'Racial Disadvantage', published in August 1981 dealt with a somewhat broader issue than the educational achievement of ethnic minority pupils. It pointed out the damaging effects of high unemployment and in particular its disproportionate impact on ethnic minorities. The Report spelled out what it regarded as a dangerous situation for contemporary British society:

> The dangers concern above all those young Asian and West Indians for the most part born in this country caught in the clash between the sometimes grim realities of their situation and their own and their parents' expectations. Far too many Asian and West Indian youngsters are unemployed, unskilled, unqualified and disenchanted, and it is above all to this problem that Parliament and the nation must address itself. (p. vii)

The Report also argued that ethnic minorities, particularly those of Caribbean origin and those originating from the Indian sub-continent, experience these disadvantages – bad housing, unemployment, educational underachievement, a deprived physical environment, social tensions – to a greater extent than the rest of the population. It pointed out that ethnic minority children, born in this country, inherited these disadvantages. In terms of educational provision, the Report commented that Asian and West Indian children encounter major difficulties in their progress through the British educational system which are not shared by white children in the same schools.

The Report identified two crucial aspects of disadvantage suffered by ethnic minorities: education and employment. Even before the publication of this government Report, a growing public concern over the question of ethnicity and educational achievement led to the creation in 1979 by the then Secretary of Education of a Committee of Inquiry into the Education of Children from Ethnic Minority Groups. The Interim Report, dubbed by the media as the Rampton Report (DES, 1981), attempted to examine the experiences of ethnic minority pupils. In spite of its unfortunate title, 'West Indian children in our [*sic*] schools', the Report contains some useful data on school achievement by West Indian pupils in Britain. It centred on the situation of West Indian children and catalogued many of the social and educational disadvantages they experienced within British society. The Committee concluded that:

> We have identified no single cause for the underachievement of West Indian children but rather a network of widely differing *attitudes* and *expectations* on the part of teachers and the educational system as a whole and on the part of West Indian parents which lead the West Indian child to have particular difficulties and face particular hurdles in achieving his or her potential. (p. 72)

While illustrating those problems, many of which may have been part of the common experience of many ethnic minority children, the Interim Report did nothing to discourage the view that reduced such children to a restrictive 'non-white' or 'black' stereotype that was developing in the minds of many people. Furthermore, the Interim Report failed to deal with factors outside the educational system in any detail. However, soon after the publication of the Interim Report, the Committee Chairman was replaced by Lord Swann, the committee subsequently being referred to as the Swann Committee. This committee published its report on 14 March 1985.

THE IMMEDIATE CONTEXT

The research reported here, the first phase of which began in 1977, looked at ethnic minority youngsters in the Leeds/Bradford area of West Yorkshire as they prepared to leave school to seek employment or further education. It seemed to have greater and wider relevance as the Interim (Rampton) Report was published.

The Leeds/Bradford area has a sizeable ethnic minority population whose origins lie in or trace back to many parts of South Asia as well as different parts of the West Indies. The findings from the first and second phases (Verma, 1981; 1982) of this longitudinal study pointed to a number of weaknesses in the Rampton Report (DES, 1981) which was drawing criticism from various quarters. The Report had a focus which did not allow for what many considered to be important socio-cultural variations among the different ethnic minority groups and which seemed likely to bear on the ethnic minority pupils' attitude towards schooling and to their educational achievement. Secondly, and this emerged as the Interim Report gained increasing publicity, the Report's findings rested too heavily on anecdotal and experiential evidence rather than on hard evidence built up from an integration of qualitative and quantitative sources.

By this time patterns emerging from our research with regard to the educational achievement of ethnic minority pupils gave us the impetus to enter a third phase in the study. This phase was designed to clarify certain factors relating to the experience of those youngsters. Phases one and two had concentrated on schooling as a preparation for work or higher education; the third phase sought to concentrate on the impact of school processes. All three phases took account of various school, community, home and personal factors that influence the individual's perception of his/her world, and especially, the individual's educational achievement. The data were analysed on a model (Chapter 6) that attempted to take into account all those inter-related factors. Examination of the literature shows that issues concerning educational achievement are far from clear. Briefly reviewing and discussing some of the personal views provided us with a new insight into the differential achievement of various ethnic groups.

The research and its findings which are reported in this book (as well as the results from the earlier phase of the studies) seek to complement the work of both the Rampton Committee and the Swann Committee. The Swann Report, despite the constraints it faced, has offered a view of the very real problems faced by black and Asian people in Britain. What this research seeks to add to that report is an appreciation of the important social, cultural, economic and individual variations that mediate the educational achievement of ethnic minority pupils. Without there being an awareness of the impact of such factors on the behaviour of the individual, there can be only imperfect progress towards the creation of a better society that is truly plural and that offers equality of educational outcome to all.

This book therefore reports a study which sought to examine the nature and process of educational aspirations, achievement and occupational success of young people from a variety of ethnic minorities attending schools in Leeds and Bradford. In the first two phases young people were studied longitudinally between the ages of 15 and 18 to assess the influence of aspiration, social and family background and examination successes upon various outcomes following the first round of public examinations. These outcomes include: examination performance; success or failure in the search for work; staying on at school; entering further education; or entering a youth training scheme. Reference to the principal findings and recommendations arising from those two phases will provide a useful framework in which to view the study as a whole.

The research in the first phase showed that the South Asian sample had significantly higher educational aspiration scores in comparison with their white counterparts. However, this was not evidence of over-aspiration on the part of the South Asian youth, as the correlation between their aspiration scores and examination grades was positive and statistically significant. Such a relationship was not found for the white sample. There was no evidence in the research that South Asians underachieved, as compared to their white counterparts.

With regard to pupils' attitude toward school education and achievement motivation it was found that the South Asian youngsters had a more positive attitude towards education and also, a higher achievement motivation than their white counterparts. These findings might be explained in terms of culturally determined values derived from the country of origin; these would include the perception of educational qualifications as a vehicle for success in life. South Asian adolescents showed a greater preference for two school subjects, Science and Mathematics, than their white peers. Occupational mobility was found to be of greater concern for the South Asian group than the white group.

Results showed that the first generation South Asians (i.e. those children born in South Asia) had a significantly higher self-esteem than the white pupils. Their higher self-esteem in spite of educational and social disadvantage, was perhaps due to the fact that the adaptation processes of first generation South Asians were mediated through the networks of family and friends, and to some extent by community-based self-help systems.

The findings and explanations of many researchers that higher educational and vocational aspirations of South Asian adolescents are due to parental influence were not confirmed by the data in phase one of this research.

A majority of our South Asian sample anticipated difficulties in achieving their goals, although they seemed highly motivated and were anxious to succeed in academic work. This high motivation set in the context of the socialisation system may partly account for the currency of the concept of over-aspiration. The research findings also clearly indicated that the careers teaching on the school curriculum was one which received scant attention in many schools, and appeared to have had little impact on most South Asian pupils.

While phase one of the research focused on young South Asians, many of its recommendations had relevance for both white school-leavers and those from different ethnic minority groups. The current climate of industrial recession makes the recommendations of that study of even greater significance:

1. There should be a greater allocation of funds to Local Authorities, the Further Education Sector and to the Manpower Services Commission to enable the expansion of facilities for education and employment.
2. There is a need for closer links between employers, educational institutions/establishments and those agencies responsible for Community Relations in order to safeguard and promote the interests of ethnic minorities.
3. It is necessary to involve ethnic minority organisations in the dissemination of information about careers opportunities, so that the parents of ethnic minority school-leavers could provide more informed and balanced advice to their children.
4. The relation of ethnic groups to each other needs to be much more closely studied. There was evidence in this research of some prejudice between the various ethnic groups themselves.
5. It is not sufficient to consider the nature of careers provision in upper schools. The findings showed that the middle school can greatly influence the choice of subjects selected by the pupil for study in the upper school. Indeed the 'die can often be cast' before a child ever begins at upper school – he or she is channelled into a certain range of subjects which determines the pupil's fortunes in the upper school.
6. The careers service plays a crucial role in helping young people to make the transition from school to work successfully. Local Education Authorities need to adopt measures to ensure that the

careers service is equipped to deal with the special needs of young South Asians for careers guidance and help in obtaining suitable employment. It is essential that careers officers are fully acquainted with the cultural background of ethnic minority pupils. There should be more training courses for Careers Officers available at both Local and national level.

The second phase of the research made a detailed, in-depth study of over 200 young people from the first phase. These young people were interviewed some three years after the start of the first phase of the research. By this time they had all passed through the first phase of public examinations at 16 or 17, had either begun study in sixth form or further education or entered (or sought to enter) the world of work. This second sample was stratified so as to include 30 per cent white and 70 per cent ethnic minority youngsters.

Throughout this research we found that individual perception of personal cause and effect differed from what seemed to be the objective reality. It can be revealing, however, to contrast two perceptions of the same subject; so we investigated both the experiences of young adults who had recently left school, and also the perceptions and experiences of all those closely involved with them such as teachers, parents, careers officers and employers.

The results of the second phase of the research were based on the analysis of both quantitative and qualitative data. These are summarised below:

1. Unemployment was higher amongst South Asians (38 per cent) than amongst the white group (23 per cent).
2. Only 9 per cent of the white group were still in further education compared to 41 per cent of the ethnic minority group.
3. A discrepancy between vocational aspiration and actual job attained was found which showed that only a few members of the cohort had actually achieved their initial ambitions. The size of this discrepancy was much greater amongst the ethnic minority group.
4. The white group studied had significantly higher self-esteem that the South Asian group.
5. Youngsters who failed to achieve their aspirations had significantly lower self-esteem than those who were able to attain these.

6.	The ethnic minority group tended, in contrast to the earlier research, to be more alienated from society and school as compared to their white counterparts.

7.	It was found that the first generation South Asians had significantly higher self-esteem than either the second generation South Asians or the white group. Both the experience of, and the prospect of unemployment seemed to have diminished the self-confidence of the South Asian group observed in an earlier phase of the research.

8.	The unemployed had lower self-esteem than the employed, and unemployment affected the individual in a potentially damaging manner. This was true for all ethnic groups.

9.	Data showed that unemployed youngsters tended to rationalise the situation by attributing the reason to factors such as the school curriculum, racial discrimination, teacher expectations and the prevailing unemployment situation in West Yorkshire, although a significant number blamed themselves for their failure to find work.

10.	The majority of our sample found careers teaching extremely inadequate and unhelpful, although some youngsters mentioned that they had received some help from the Authority's careers officers. Most members of the cohort had experienced various kinds of difficulty in their transition from school to work/further education.

Having sketched out the general and immediate contexts of this study, it is now appropriate to consider its objectives, operational strategies and the framework employed to analyse the data that it generated.

6 Research Objectives, Analytical Framework and Operational Techniques

The main concern throughout this research has been to explore the educational achievement of major ethnic groups in British schools, and to identify factors influencing their achievement and underachievement. In this chapter we examine methodological issues relating to the research framework and the techniques used in order to seek answers to the research questions. It should be pointed out that methodological choices are usually made for theoretical, philosophical and pragmatic reasons that have little to do with the expected nature of the research findings. Yet, the methodological considerations provide an insight into the different dimensions of the study.

RESEARCH OBJECTIVES

Phase One

'Aspiration' was the main focus in this phase. One of the factors behind its usage was that the literature on ethnic minorities in the British educational system tends to confine itself to the description of features of particular cultures. It rarely attempts to explain the way in which education operates in the consciousness of different ethnic groups in society. Now that Britain is a multicultural, multi-ethnic society, the implications of such a deficiency are profound.

Studies have consistently shown that Asians and West Indians suffer from multiple disadvantage in British society (Smith, 1976; Mackintosh and Smith, 1974; CRE, 1978) and restricted employment. It has also been demonstrated that disadvantages experienced by some individuals in early life can profoundly affect their success at the later stages of schooling (see, for example, Rutter *et al.*, 1979). When an individual's aspirations are high but likely to be disappointed, there may be serious socio-psychological consequences for the adaptation of the individual to working life (Verma, 1982). It can also be argued that the adaptation processes of first generation immigrants are mediated through a diffuse network of friends, family and community-based self-help systems; whilst children of immigrants are exposed both to their parents' culture and to those socialisation agencies, particularly school and peer group, which serve the native British community.

However, for the native British youth the values of home and school are likely to be broadly consistent with those of society at large. For the new generation of black and Asian British youngsters, the degree of congruence cannot be assumed; it is likely to be subject to variation in ways which are significant for the process of educational and occupational adaptation. It cannot be assumed either that congruence is achieved entirely by adjustments on the part of ethnic minority populations. In this phase of research, particular attention was paid to factors determining educational adaptation, and the relationship between vocational choices and cultural continuity within the community and the family.

Brody (1969) rightly comments that 'adaptation in the psychological sense refers to the process of establishing and maintaining a relatively stable reciprocal relationship with the environment.' Where this 'environment' is predominantly social, the term adaptation loses some of its Darwinian overtones, and may form the basis of an 'interactionist' model for understanding human behaviour. In examining the educational adaptation of ethnic minority teenagers we believed that such a perspective would be preferable to the more usual concept of 'assimilation' which implies a one-way process.

The process of adaptation is determined by the past experience, present state and future expectations of the individual. Moreover, adaptation to urban life is not a unitary process. It involves a period of acute insecurity and anxiety as demonstrated for example by Richmond's study (1967) of British and other immigrants to Canada. Thus, the process of settling down in the new cultural environment and establishing satisfactory relationships between one's traditional values, beliefs and attitudes and those prevalent in the dominant culture is an extremely difficult one. In this research adolescents' hopes for the future (careers preparation) were examined as a means of assessing the broader implications of the adaptation to life in Britain of ethnic minority communities.

The concept of differential aspiration was first introduced by Beetham (1967) in discussion of aspiration on the part of ethnic minorities in Britain, particularly 'Asians'. According to him, 'Asians' aspire to occupations which require qualifications 'beyond their reach'. He attributes this to various causes, one of them being the cultural factor. Other studies have also discussed the relevance of cultural influences on educational and occupational expectations of ethnic minority youngsters (e.g. Gupta, 1977; Fowler *et al.*, 1977; Baker, 1978; CRE, 1978). As a result of such studies 'culturally determined' over-aspiration and underachievement have become a prevailing conceptual orthodoxy. What is lacking in most studies is an adequate treatment of the way in which aspirations are constructed. One of the main objectives in our research was to investigate the ways in which ethnic minority youngsters' aspirations are different from those of indigenous teenagers, and to demonstrate the inadequacy of a bi-polar approach to aspirations in terms of 'high' and 'low' levels. The qualities which differentiate the aspirations of ethnic minority adolescents from those of indigenous teenagers are multi-dimensional, and reflect the complexity of the social situation facing migrants and their children from the Third World in Western metropolitan society.

In our research we have also been concerned with casting a wide net over the factors determining educational adaptation, and the relationships between vocational choices and cultural continuity within the complex set of social forces. The following broad questions formed the basis of the first phase of our research:

(a) do ethnic minority youngsters underachieve compared to their white counterparts?
(b) how far are their educational aspirations in line with their levels of achievement, again in comparison with their white peers?
(c) what factors influence those aspirations?
(d) to what extent do teachers and careers officers perceive ethnic minority youngsters in negative or positive terms?
(e) to what extent do employers perceive black and Asian youngsters in those terms?
(f) to what extent do these youngsters come into conflict with an education system which may not provide them with 'qualifications' to enable them to compete with their white peers?

(g)   what are the values inherent in the normative conception of a 'correct' level of educational aspiration?
(h)   to what extent does the British educational system discourage the expectations of working class British adolescents?
(i)   to what extent does the British education system act as a filtering process by which the system of social stratification is reproduced?

Phase Two

This phase was primarily designed to continue research into the cohort of adolescents identified and investigated during the first phase. By examining this group longitudinally it was hoped, firstly to examine the occupational experience of adolescents of different ethnic origins, and secondly to set these experiences in the context of environmental and cultural variables. These variables included the previously determined ones of achievement aspirations, educational achievement and expectations of working life.

While the research was in progress a most important environmental change began which was to cause a shift in the direction of our investigations. The rise in unemployment which particularly affected school-leavers and ethnic minorities (the 'target groups' of the research) necessitated an expansion of the scope of the study to include both the personal consequences of unemployment and the process of adapting to it. This allowed comparisons to be made between employed and unemployed youngsters and hence deepened insight into the processes involved in the transition from school to work. Every member of the cohort was either unemployed or had a friend or relation who was, and this affected the perception of these youngsters of the working environment.

The research objectives in this phase were:

(a)   to monitor and evaluate career paths – whether individuals had rejected the critical imperatives of their background, or developed alternative directions;
(b)   to educe the relationship between aspirations and subsequent occupational placement across ethnic groups;
(c)   to evaluate the impact of the workplace on the individual's cultural perspective;
(d)   to evaluate the impact of success or failure on the individual's identity in respect of career aspirations;

(e) to learn whether failure is attributed to discrimination, and the impact this has on the individual's adjustment to working life;
(f) to learn whether racial discrimination is a major factor in determining the occupational placement of ethnic minority youth in Britain;
(g) to identify differences across ethnic groups in patterns of occupational selection;
(h) to identify the effects of unemployment and learn whether these effects are similar for each ethnic group.

Phase Three

The third phase of this longitudinal study was designed to gain an insight into the differential educational achievement of ethnic minority adolescents. During the first phase when the initial data were collected, unemployment was not as great a problem for school leavers as it has since become. It would therefore have been invalid to interpret these data as being representative of the attitudes and experiences of youngsters in 1983. Here our aim was to evaluate the school-leaving process for youngsters in the light of hypotheses derived from the previous two phases. Thus greater emphasis was given to the role of educational achievement in the transition process than before.

A major change which could be identified from an initial review of the area was the increased number of youngsters who stayed on at school. Therefore it was decided to analyse, among other things, the reasons why some pupils left school whilst others stayed on, even though their formal qualifications were often similar. Apart from the reduced scale of this phase of our investigations, the rationale remained broadly unchanged from the earlier ones. The additional data were useful in identifying trends, and testing some of the hypotheses raised by the earlier research.

Thus, this phase of the research stemmed from both the current debate about the role of education in social and occupational mobility, and from the longitudinal research over the period 1977–1982 (phases one and two). It was hoped to establish profiles of high and low achievers among adolescents within different ethnic groups. From these profiles it was intended to ascertain what differences existed across these groups and to highlight the educational, social, cultural and individual factors and processes that mediated upon them.

Profiles of high and low achievers within major ethnic groups were subjected to analysis on three levels:

(a) *Cultural factors*
   (i) composition of various cultures;
  (ii) some 'core values' of each culture;
 (iii) the individual's perception of his/her group membership and others' view of this.
(b) *Immediate environment of the individual*
     Family, school, peers and other environmental variables were studied, and how they interacted to produce cultural factors.
(c) *Individual factors*
     Analysis for this level included self-esteem, motivation, attitude and language use.

ANALYTICAL FRAMEWORK

All too often there is a tendency for one particular type of social scientist, working within his or her own discipline, to attempt to explain a particular phenomenon without reference to the other perspectives which are available. In this research the separate perspectives were taken as complementary in a three-level system of analysis in order to gain an insight into the achievement process. The first level sought to establish the wider social situation of the ethnic groups in Britain, including social class, levels of unemployment, under-employment, housing and so on. Analysis of relative achievement in terms of the wider social situation of ethnic minorities was useful in establishing the relationship between social and educational disadvantage. The second level of analysis attempted to establish the 'immediate environment' of the youngsters through which the wider social considerations are mediated. The 'immediate environment' concerns factors such as family, school, and peer group which are likely to bear on the process of achievement. The third level was concerned with the psychology of the individual pupils; here the focus was on factors which might be affected by the 'immediate environment' and those which might affect the youngsters' achievement in the examination room. The relationship of the three levels is outlined diagramatically in Figure 6.1.

Brief mention should be made of the nature and relevance of each of the three levels.

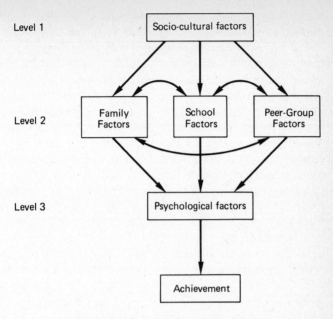

Level 1 — Socio-cultural factors

Level 2 — Family Factors / School Factors / Peer-Group Factors

Level 3 — Psychological factors

Achievement

FIGURE 6.1   *The levels of analysis*

There is sufficient evidence to suggest that ethnic minorities in Britain suffer disproportionately from both unemployment and underemployment. A survey by the Runnymede Trust (1981) showed that the overall proportion of black and Asian people without a job (as a proportion of all unemployed people) had increased from 2.4 per cent in 1972 to 4 per cent in 1981. Secondly, between 1972 and 1981 it showed that total national unemployment had increased by 138 per cent whereas black and Asian unemployment had increased by 325 per cent. Thirdly, the number of unemployed school-leavers increased at over twice the national average for all workers; this increase was even greater for ethnic minority youngsters. Fourthly, unemployment amongst the under-25 age group increased faster for blacks and Asians than for whites. The survey also found that British-born blacks and Asians had higher levels of unemployment than those who had immigrated to Britain. This was most surprising since ethnic minorities born in Britain would have received all their education within the British educational system.

There is also a considerable body of evidence which shows that ethnic minorities are generally '*under*employed' as well (Smith, 1976; 1981). It is also true that immigrants tend to settle, out of necessity, in inner-city areas where housing is cheap. This may, however, mean that schools attended by ethnic minority pupils have fewer educational resources, for 'good' schools tend to be situated in middle-class suburban areas (Acton, 1981). This combination of unemployment, underemployment and the attendant consequences for housing and income levels is at the heart of multiple disadvantage. Such issues provide the basis of a context in which to view educational achievement, and one which prepares the way for an understanding of the immediate environment.

The second level of our model is concerned with the 'immediate' environment of the individual. There is no dearth of evidence to suggest that school has an important part to play in the achievement process of pupils (Rutter *et al.*, 1979; Stone, 1981). Driver (1977) found that the 'cultural incompetence' of many teachers in British schools and their failure to find an appropriate teaching style for the multi-ethnic context are associated with the underachievement of ethnic minority pupils; Driver emphasised the relationships within the school, particularly between teacher and pupil, arguing that increased inter-cultural understanding is essential for learning.

Evidence that the peer group can mediate upon the educational adaptation of teenagers has been provided by Willis (1977) amongst others. The results showed that the sub-cultural pressures of peer group and immediate family can reduce educational aspiration and consequently achievement motivation among youngsters to bring them down to an 'acceptable level'. Most studies in this area which examine the peer-group influence have concentrated upon the ethnic constitution of such groups (e.g. Jelinek and Brittan, 1975; they suggest that intra-ethnic peer groups are the general rule, though not entirely to the exclusion of all ethnically dissimilar individuals.

The prevailing stereotypes and naive assumptions concerning the family life of the major ethnic groups in British society are that all Asians live in extended families, the native whites live in nuclear families and West Indians live in one-parent families. Such judgements about life-styles of ethnic groups are not only loaded but ethnocentric. Assuming that such stereotypes hold some truth (and this is a big assumption!), care must be taken not to hold alternative family styles responsible for differential educational achievement. Currently at least there is no body of evidence of any substance to support the link. After all, family patterns are derived to some extent from the area of origin. Therefore the research which has shown a tendency for immigrant groups to move towards the nuclear family (Rex and Tomlinson, 1979) may have no bearing on future trends in academic achievement of those groups.

Bagley and his associates (1979) found that working-class Jamaican parents in particular tended to have high regard for the education process, and also held an authoritarian attitude to child-rearing. They have argued that this combination of attitudes has led some Jamaican parents to suppress individuality and reinforce conformity, both of which seem to help the child to succeed in the Jamaican education system. The authors have pointed out that these characteristics are no longer held imperative by the British education system. Thus it becomes possible that the values upheld in the home and at school may be in conflict, the outcome being that children are pushed into the security of their peer group. Nevertheless, it is difficult to speculate about the extent of such influences upon the achievement of pupils at the age of sixteen and beyond.

In this research, the influences of school, peer group and family were used to build up a picture of the 'immediate' environment of the individual. It cannot be assumed, however, that these influences are equal for every individual regardless of whether overall cultural differences exist or not. It must be recognised that individual differences may occur in the immediate environment which may overshadow cultural influences for any individual. Nevertheless, the broad aspects within the immediate environment have formed the second level of analysis of the achievement process.

The third level of analysis in our research is concerned with psychological factors. One such factor implicated in the achievement process is self-esteem. Although Bagley, Mallick and Verma (1979) attribute most of the influence of self-esteem on educational achievement to the 'general self' component (i.e. self-esteem not derived from a specific social situation), its components are also derived from interactions and relationships within the home, the school and the peer group (Coopersmith, 1967). Thus a useful working hypothesis is that self-esteem is a mediatory factor between the immediate environment and educational achievement.

There are a number of issues associated with the measurement of self-esteem in general which should be borne in mind when examining research evidence concerning self-esteem across cultures (see Bagley, Verma, Mallick and Young, 1979). Studies in Britain on self-concept and self-esteem amongst ethnic minority children and adolescents have produced findings both diverse and contradictory. However, self-esteem is crucially important in individual functioning, and that global identity is an overriding concept in which self-esteem is subsumed.

Another psychological factor implicated in the achievement process is concerned with 'locus of control'. Essentially this is a personality variable which conceptualises the fact that some people (externalisers) tend to explain what happens to them in terms of factors beyond their control, whilst others (internalisers) believe that events are the result of their own actions. Louden (1978) points out that externalisers are more likely to have their self-esteem affected by events within the immediate environment than are internalisers. Louden found that West Indian youngsters tended to be more external in their locus of control than either South Asian or English youngsters. This aspect of the psychological dimension is important in considering the achievement process, because it would seem to have some bearing on the impact of the immediate environment for individuals and groups of individuals.

The final psychological factor included in our research is concerned with pupils' motivation at school and more specifically their motive to achieve. Two aspects of achievement motivation have been included in our analysis: the hope of success (HS) which represents the individual's striving to achieve because of the rewards it gives; and the fear of failure (FF) which represents the individual's defence reaction to the psychological effect of failure (Clark, Teevan and Riccuitti, 1955). Achievement motivation, particularly the balance between the two aspects, would appear to be closely related to the self-esteem of the individual.

The 'levels of analysis' approach to the examination of educational achievement as outlined above represents an attempt at a comprehensive means of viewing the situation. However, as with the classification of ethnicity, it is a tool which may or may not be useful in understanding the processes of achievement across ethnic groups. These processes are necessarily complex and any model developed to map out the frame of reference of research must attempt to continue each and every valid perspective of the problem. It is hoped that the model outlined above will serve to clarify the multi-disciplinary approach adopted in this research.

Discussion of the analytical model would be incomplete if we did not set out here the rationale used for looking at educational achievement itself. The direction of our thinking in that respect will have already become apparent from our consideration of educational achievement and ethnicity in Chapter Four.

Much of the debate over why certain individuals or groups of individuals perform poorly centres on what the school is doing or not doing. Educational achievement is not simply the fulfilment of intellectual potential as measured by performance in public examinations. Such a criterion overlooks two important considerations.

Firstly, educational achievement is the outcome of a complex process involving factors within an individual's environment. Unlike previous studies in the field, this research was concerned with the relative performance of groups of individuals and the factors which affect their performance, rather than concentrating on the relative contribution to performance of the school attended. Only in this way can one get to the heart of the processes leading to achievement.

Secondly, to concentrate on the measurement of educational achievement by performance in public examinations – although an important criterion – overlooks the performance of a considerable part of the school population in its last year of compulsory schooling. Public examinations are designed to cater for approximately the top 60 per cent of 16-year-olds, although perhaps as many as 85 per cent of them attempt examination entry in one or two subjects. Thus examination performance itself is too simplistic a measure of educational achievement.

For this reason, further criteria of educational achievement had to be adopted in order that an effective analysis could be made of the factors contributing to achievement. Four indicators of the educational process were employed: examination results, occupational entry, self-esteem and the youngster's assessment of his or her own achievement.

The reasons for adopting the first indicator are self evident. Occupational entry was adopted because although very often relating closely to educational success it does offer a measure of achievement that extends beyond pure 'academic' success. Self-esteem was adopted because, despite its associations with examination success, it also offers a broad indicator of social adjustment, which is an important part in the purpose and process of schooling. The fourth indicator relates closely to self-esteem and social adjustment. The youngster's assessment of his or her own achievement is a more sensitive and personal indicator of achievement than that of academic success; one *can* enjoy school and leave school well adjusted socially yet with no passes in public examinations.

These indicators were by no means exhaustive but offered a broader insight than that offered by examination results alone into differential performance at school and the impact of schooling on individual pupils.

There are difficulties in determining the level of achievement which may be regarded as 'normal' for each pupil. Furthermore, the term 'underachievement' appears to have two distinct meanings depending upon the context in which it is used. When referring to an individual pupil, 'underachievement' has been taken to mean that the pupil has not realised his potential or reached that 'normal' or expected level of performance; the pupil is being compared against a set of his own personal attributes which implies that he should have done better. When used in reference to groups of pupils, 'underachievement' is taken to mean that the target group is achieving at a lower level than another group, which for some reason is taken as representative of 'normal' achievement. It is important to recognise the dissimilarity between the origins of the two usages. If a certain group of pupils tends to achieve less than another group it does not necessarily imply that all members of the low achieving group are failing to realise their own potential. Failure to appreciate this distinction may result in the erroneous belief that all those in a low achieving group are underachieving, or are likely to do so on the individual level.

In this research, the term 'underachievement' has not been used. At no stage have the youngsters in the study been compared with external measures of their potential. Comparison across ethnic groups has been kept to a minimum in respect of achievement scores by utilising *intra*-ethnic analysis rather than *inter*-ethnic analysis. The term 'underachievement' therefore has little meaning under either of the definitions outline above.

It was stated at the outset that this research sought to offer an insight into the social and psychological processes which may influence the educational achievement of youngsters from various groups in Britain. Such an aim is *not* equatable with the attempt to determine why one ethnic group may appear to underachieve and another not. One intention of this research was to attempt to offer strategies to offset educational disadvantage faced by ethnic minorities in Britain. Thus it was not considered necessary to map out the factors contributing to disadvantage, which have been outlined proficiently by others (see

Smith, 1976). It was considered more important to seek to arrive at an understanding of the processes which lead to achievement for each group under study. Comparison across ethnic groups (inter-ethnic analysis) may well facilitate the identification of factors contributing to educational disadvantage. However, it offers relatively little help in understanding the social and psychological processes that operate within a particular culture.

The inter-ethnic research strategy entails the collection of data on samples from two or more ethnic groups, the data being comprised of factors which may be linked to the achievement process and could include personal, educational, familial or demographic measures. The data are then analysed in a manner which compares across the broadly defined cultural groups on each of the variables within the data set. This is carried out to ascertain on which, if any, of the variables a significant difference exists between the groups. If a difference in educational achievement between the groups has also been established, it may then be concluded that the difference in educational achievement is the consequence of differences on the other variables. At first sight this may seem a legitimate approach; however, it is based on the assumption that a factor will affect culturally distinct groups in a similar manner. Unless steps have been taken to establish that each variable has a similar effect on the members of each cultural group, there is the risk of serious errors of interpevration being made.

The intra-cultural research strategy makes no such assumptions. The data collection was conducted in a similar manner but the criterion of analysis is somewhat different. Within the analysis no attempt is made to compare between ethnic groups; instead each ethnic group is sub-divided into 'high achievers' and 'low achievers' by comparison with the median achievement level for that ethnic group. Analysis then proceeds to determine (for each ethnic group separately) those factors relating to the distinction between high and low achievement. This yields a list of factors which relate to achievement for a particular group. If the factors so obtained are very similar for each ethnic group, then the inter-ethnic analysis outlined above would be justified. If the factors are dissimilar then it must be accepted that the processes which lead to educational achievement may be culture-specific and not open to ethnocentric interpretation based upon a conventional analysis of the mainstream culture.

One of the benefits of intra-ethnic analysis is that it does not lend itself to the reinforcement of existing stereotypes concerning the relative achievement of ethnic groups in Britain. For example, teacher expectation that West Indian pupils in particular are likely to achieve poorly at school has been identified by the Rampton enquiry:

> Again it has repeatedly been pointed out to us that low expectations of the academic ability of West Indian pupils by teachers can often prove a self-fulfilling prophecy. Many teachers feel that West Indians are unlikely to achieve in academic terms but may have high expectations of their potential in areas such as sport, dance, drama and art. If these particular skills are unduly emphasised there is a risk of establishing a view of West Indian children that may become a stereotype and teachers may be led to encourage pupils to pursue these subjects at the expense of their academic studies.
>
> (HMSO, 1981, p. 13)

Intra-ethnic analysis has been used previously by Bagley, Bart and Wong (1979) in their study of the antecedents of scholastic success in West Indian ten-year-olds in London. They found that, in general, those who were achieving well at school:

> had parents who are highly critical of English culture, and the English educational system . . . a positive attitude to school as a medium for achievement, and a positive ethnic self-image.
>
> (Bagley, Bart and Wong, 1979, p. 93)

These authors clearly imply that identification with the traditional cultural values of the ethnic group helps children to achieve during their formative years. Had these researchers employed an inter-ethnic research strategy it is highly unlikely that these factors would have emerged, since high achieving English children are unlikely to have parents who are critical of 'English' culture. Here, the antecedents of achievement were certainly culture-based and there is little reason to suppose that these factors affected each ethnic group similarly.

The concept of 'underachievement' can only appear therefore when one has established what is 'normal' achievement, either by reference to the ability of the pupil or to a comparison group of pupils. When using intra-ethnic analysis, which does not make use of either comparison, the term no longer has meaning. The preferred terms in this research are 'relatively high-achieving' and 'relatively low-achieving', being defined by whether the pupil or group of pupils fall above or below the median for that particular ethnic group.

OPERATIONAL TECHNIQUES USED

Phase One

(*a*)   *The Vocational Adaptation Questionnaire*

The questionnaire used in the first phase of research was intended to cast a wide net over a large number of issues concerning the educational aspirations and expectations of young people from different ethnic backgrounds. It was administered orally to 1036 pupils from the fifth forms of the five schools in Bradford and the two schools in Leeds which participated in this study.

The information obtained by use of this questionnaire included, among others, the following aspects: area where the respondent lived; area of origin with amount of schooling overseas; language spoken at home; liking for school subjects; examination intentions; extra-curricular activities; hobbies, if any; intentions on leaving school; job aspirations; higher education aspirations; difficulties anticipated in achieving ambitions; perceived parental influence and interest; peer-group influence; perceived importance of job attributes; influence of careers teaching in school; school experience in general; teacher attitudes and so on.

(*b*)   *The Shortened Vocational Adaptation Questionnaire*

A shortened form of the vocational adaptation questionnaire was administered to a reduced sample of 220 pupils at the second level of research in Phase One. They were randomly selected and interviewed individually. This questionnaire was designed in such a way that it could be completed in a shorter time than the large questionnaire and relied to a greater extent on 'multiple choice' questions. The range of issues covered was narrower than within the larger questionnaire and attempted greater depth in specific areas, such as: type of jobs liked and reasons; any specific jobs not wanted and reasons; difficulties anticipated in getting the job wanted; parental influence in the choice of jobs; further education aspired to, and so on. Since some six months had elapsed since the administration of the first questionnaire it was felt necessary to reassess the opinions and attitudes of the youngsters.

(c)   *The Pupil Interview Schedule (see Appendix 2)*

The purpose of the interview at the second level of Phase One was to augment the questionnaire responses, not to replace them. A semi-structured interview schedule was designed to obtain as free a response as possible over a wide range of issues relating to educational and occupational aspirations, together with a number of other variables, e.g. social class, ethnic/cultural background. This approach was considered preferable to the prescription of a set of detailed questions, which would tend to constrict the range of responses.

One of the limitations often mentioned about interview techniques is that the researcher interprets the data by giving it a meaning that may not be warranted by the data but reflects his/her biases or theoretical framework. Another problem, specific to this research, concerns the matching or mismatching of ethnic background between the interviewer and the respondent. In order to reduce the effect of these problems, interviewers from both indigenous white and ethnic minority backgrounds interviewed a few youngsters independently. Analysis of transcribed interview data was carried out by two researchers independently.

(d)   *The Coopersmith Self-Esteem Inventory*

This 58-item inventory provides a general assessment of self-esteem which may be broken down into the following component sub-scales:

1.   General-Self measure (how the individual perceives himself)
2.   Social measure (how the individual perceives himself socially)
3.   Home measure (how the individual perceives his home life)
4.   School measure (how the individual perceives his school life)
5.   Lie-scale (a measure of how truthfully the individual has performed on the inventory).

The inventory was developed by Coopersmith, and its reliability and validity have been established (Coopersmith, 1967). It has also been used cross-culturally in American and British studies (Coopersmith, 1967; Verma, 1975; Bagley, Verma, Mallick and Young, 1979; Bagley, Mallick and Verma, 1979). The respondent is asked to put a tick in the column 'like me' if the item describes how he/she feels. If the item does not describe how he/she feels the respondent is asked to put a tick in the column 'unlike me'. Instructions also state that there are no right and wrong answers.

In the test sample items are:

1. I spend a lot of time day-dreaming.
2. Someone always has to tell me what to do.
30. It's pretty tough to be me.
50. I don't care what happens to me.
56. I often get discouraged in school.

The test is scored by totalling the 'like me' and 'unlike me' responses for each scale, and then (for the total-scale score) adding these together. The composite score then gives a measure of individuals' self-esteem which varies between 0 and 100 since 50 items are scored (8 Lie-Scale items are excluded in the final score). The General-Self component varies between 0 and 52 (i.e. 52 items), whilst the other 3 sub-scales vary between 0 and 16 (i.e. 8 items).

In Phase One of the research no such differentiation was made (with the exception of the lie-scale). A score by totalling the values assigned to the four sub-scales was obtained as a measure of self-esteem. However, on subsequent phases of the research, differentiation of the scores on each sub-scale was made in addition to the total self-esteem score.

Although the test has proved promising in several studies in a British setting (Bagley, Verma, Mallick and Young, 1979), a pilot study was carried out prior to the first phase of the research to determine its applicability to the age group of the sample. Statistical analysis indicated the suitability of the test for 15–18-year-olds. The set of items was also tested for comprehensibility with a group of 500 youngsters in British secondary schools.

(e) The Motive–Attitude Intensity Scale (MAIS)

This test was designed to assess several aspects of pupils' motivation in school. The author of the test (Sumner, 1971) identified two broad components in pupils' motivation, (i) motives classified as social conformity, interest and reward, (ii) attitudes relating to parents, friends, self and teachers.

The test is intended for twelve-to-sixteen-year-olds and has 140 items distributed between the scales. Each scale has been balanced for an acquiescence set. The respondent is asked to read the items carefully and to put a tick in one of the three columns (Agree, Disagree, Uncertain) which best suits his/her opinion. Sample items are:

1.   Teachers always give high marks for good work.
10.   Most of my friends look on school as a drag.
37.   I try to understand how to improve my standards.
47.   I do not know what I am aiming at at school.
122. There is no need to join in at sports because other people do.

The reliability, validity, internal stability of the concepts and consistency of responses have been established in various ways (Sumner, 1969).

A slightly modified version of the scale was used in the present research. The information from pupils' responses to items was obtained in the form of a total score for the general level of motivation to school education. The assumption behind the rationale of this scale is that high scoring pupils will do 'better' in their school work. Use of the MAIS was limited to the first phase of the research, partly because the time required for its completion precludes its use with a large number of pupils.

(f)   Assessment of Achievement Motivation

The work of McClelland and his associates (1953) on a group Thematic Apperceptions Test (TAT) measure of need for achievement (nAch) produced evidence suggesting that this measure involves two distinct aspects of achievement motivation: hope of success (HS) and fear of failure (FF). HS is an approach motive involving anticipation of reward (motive to achieve), and FF is an avoidance motive involving participation of punishment (motive to avoid failure). This distinction was later confirmed by other researchers (Mawer, 1960; Heckhausen, 1967). The definition of 'achievement motivation' adopted by Heckhausen was 'the individual striving to increase capacity in all activities in which some standard of excellence is thought to apply'.

The selection of stimulus material was guided by the judgements of six psychologists as well as earlier investigations in this field. Responses from four cards were utilised in this research in terms of the above aspects of achievement motivation – hope of success and fear of failure. The selected cards were:

Card No. 1 – A boy is contemplating a violin which rests on a table in front of him.

Card No. 2 – A young woman with books in her hand: in the background a man is working in the fields and an older woman is looking on.

Card No. 8 – An adolescent looks straight out of the picture. The barrel of a rifle is visible at one side and in the background is the dim scene of a surgical operation, like a reverie image.

Card No. 17 – A naked man is clinging to a rope. He is in the act of climbing up or down.

The administration procedures, and verbal instructions to the testees were adapted from those used by Argyle and Robinson (1962). Pupils were allowed thirty seconds to look at each picture and four minutes to write a story about it. Four questions as a guide in the writing of the stories were suggested:

1. What is happening? Who are these people?
2. What past events have led up to this situation?
3. What is being sought or wanted? By whom?
4. What is likely to happen next?

In evaluating the stories a modified scoring scheme derived from McClelland and his associates (1953) and Atkinson (1958) was followed. Separate scores were obtained for the HS (nAch+) and FF(nAch−) variables as distinguished by Clark, Teevan and Riccuitti (1956). Content analysis of imaginative stories was carried out to determine whether the story contained the success-oriented aspect or the failure-oriented aspect of achievement motivation. Other criteria in the scoring included intensity, frequency and duration with which these themes appeared in the stories. The final score, based on overall impression of the answer, was assigned to each story on two scales. The HS scale ranged from 5 (very high) to 1 (almost lacking), and the FF scale ranged from 1 (very high) to 5 (almost lacking). The two final scores were obtained by totalling the scores assigned to the four stories.

Validation studies of this test with pupils were carried out on 180 subjects. The results concerning the reliability and validity are published elsewhere (Verma, 1973). The reliability coefficients between the three scores on the two variables (HS and FF) ranged from 0.64 to 0.88. Similarly, intercorrelations of the combined ratings between the pictures were moderately reliable. The reliability coefficients of the combined ratings were 0.66 (HS) and 0.65 (FF).

Phase Two

(a)   *The Occupational Adaptation Questionnaire and the Interview Schedule*

The questionnaire served two purposes. Firstly, the questions were designed to enable the factual events in the pupil's last three years to be documented, and included ethnic origin, job history, parental employment and so on. Secondly, since the questionnaire was administered orally by the interviewer it offered opportunity for a rapport to be established between him/her and the youngster prior to the semi-structured and tape-recorded interview that followed.

The rationale and interview techniques were identical to the interviews conducted during the first phase of the study. Here too the interviews were tape-recorded and transcribed for analyses. The analysis itself again was conducted by two researchers independently.

(b)   *The F-Scale*

Derived from the pioneering work of Adorno and his colleagues (1950), the F-Scale attempts to educe the degree of authoritarianism in the individual. The modified version used in this study was the one produced by Himmelweit and Swift (1971). In their longitudinal study, they used attitude statements from both the original Adorno scale and Levinson's Family Ideology Scale. They have suggested that all responses to attitude statements, including authoritarian ones, should be viewed in a three-dimensional space of cognitive complexity, social structure and interpersonal relations.

The F-Scale used in the second phase of the research consisted of 25 items (Himmelweit and Swift, 1971) which are divided into four sub-scales:

1.   Authoritarian View of Society (AS): gives an indication of how the individual views the world.

2. Authoritarian Parental Rule (AP): gives an indication of what the individual believes concerning parent–child relationships.
3. Pro-conformity and Status-Quo (SQ): represents that side of the authoritarian personality which believes that change is undesirable.
4. Jaundiced View of Life (JV): represents that part of the authoritarian personality which leads to quasi-paranoic responses.

Each of the items represents a statement of a particular attitude or belief. The respondent is invited to indicate the degree to which he/she agrees or disagrees with the sentiment by reference to a five-point scale. Taken as a whole the scale may be taken as a measure of 'alienation from society'.

(*c*) *The Coopersmith Self-Esteem Inventory* was also utilised in this

phase of the research. Here however, unlike in the first phase of the research, the scale was divided into its component sub-scales in addition to the full-scale score.

Phase Three

(*a*) *The Questionnaire* (see Appendix 3)

This questionnaire facilitated a more detailed analysis of the ethnicity of the youngster than either of the earlier questionnaires. Moreover, an attempt was made to investigate the reasoning underlying specific responses. Certain questions were worded identically to those of the previous questionnaire to enable direct, unequivocal comparison between the two samples. Specific topics highlighted in the questionnaire were factors relating to achievement at school and expected reaction to the prospect of unemployment.

(*b*) *The Interview Schedule* (see Appendix 4)

A set of questions was constructed as part of semi-structured interviews with school-leavers and sixth-formers from the two schools involved in the third phase of the research. Again questions were not arranged in any specific order, the interviewer being left to present each question in a suitable moment during conversation. In this way it was hoped to stimulate normal conversation as nearly as possible within the artificial situation of the research interview. Interviewers from different ethnic backgrounds and of both sexes were used in an attempt to minimise ethnic and sexual biases.

The main issues in the interview schedule included: the experiences of the youngsters after reaching statutory school-leaving age; reasons for either leaving or staying on at school; responses to examination success or failure; views of education and the role of education in obtaining employment; opinions of the advice they had received at school pertaining to leaving and entering employment/further education.

7 Educational Achievement: Patterns and Trends

The findings of the research are presented in two parts: the first part is concerned with analysis of the quantitative data acquired by using questionnaires and standardised tests; the second is concerned with findings from the interview data and other sources. We saw the need for both qualitative field studies and quantitative data, combining the psychometric techniques with the interview data in a broad-front approach to the study. It was hoped that presenting the information from questionnaires and tests would establish the broad findings of the research in a form where decisions concerning the representativeness of the data might be made. The uniqueness of the individual experience consisting of the opinions and experiences of the youngsters was intended to give greater depth to the statistical findings which may otherwise appear impersonal. Such close scrutiny of individual cases gave us some understanding of the complexity of differential academic achievement across ethnic groups and led us away from simplistic concepts of cause and effect in the education of young people.

Throughout this chapter, the reader should be aware that mean sub-group responses represent only the average response of all the youngsters in that sub-group. Neither does the mean response necessarily represent the 'typical' response for that sub-group; more often than not adolescents will have responded either above or below the mean.

The material in the second part of this chapter does not lend itself to eliciting stereotyped responses since statements are primarily those of individuals. Nevertheless, it should also be remembered that an individual is not necessarily 'typical' of the ethnic, religious or sexual sub-group to which he/she belongs.

It will be remembered that this research was conducted in three

95

phases. The first phase (1977–79) represented studies of some 1200 youngsters of different ethnic groups prior to leaving school. The second phase (1980–82) was a follow-up on this cohort. Findings from these phases of the research are reported elsewhere (Verma and Ashworth, 1983) and the broad patterns are outlined in Chapter Five. The third phase (1982–83), reported here, was a study of 413 fifth-formers and 80 school leavers from two Bradford schools. Because of missing data in some questionnaires, 394 subjects were finally utilised in the third phase of the research.

The composition of the sample for the combined three phases of the research, drawn from nine schools, was as follows:

	White	Indian	Pakistani	Bangladeshi	West Indian	Other
Female	290	66	78	36	38	22
Male	366	90	92	44	54	48
Totals	656	156	170	80	92	70

Of the identified ethnic minorities, 80 per cent had been born in Britain. Of the South Asian group, 21 per cent were Hindu, 18 per cent were Sikh and 61 per cent were Moslem.

EXAMINATION ENTRY

In an earlier chapter we saw there was much debate about the educational achievement of ethnic minority youngsters compared to their white peers. Any differences in ethnic-group examination results may arise because certain groups tend to perform poorly in examinations or because they take fewer examination subjects initially. Analysis of the number and type of examinations the young people were expecting to take towards the end of their fifth form showed no significant differences between ethnic groups. The results showed a significant sex difference at the 5 per cent level, however, with girls tending to take more examinations than boys. Analysis of Variance (Table 7.1)* was computed to see if there was a significant interaction between ethnic group and sex. This analysis confirmed the sex difference but no other significant effect was obtained.

ANTECEDENTS OF EXAMINATION PERFORMANCE

Two techniques were used to find the factors relating to examination achievement for each ethnic group, (Tables 7.2–7.8). Firstly, *multiple*

* Tables to this chapter appear in Appendix 1, pp. 150–63.

regression of major predictor variables was used to determine how much *variance* of examination achievement was accounted for by each factor. Secondly, '*median-split*' *analysis* was used to discover which factors best separate relatively high and low achievers within each ethnic group. The results of the multiple regression analyses show that the independent factors account for different amounts of variance for different ethnic groups. Within the achieving process, then, certain factors appear important for some ethnic groups but not for others. For example, maternal interest in school performance was a major determinant of examination success for West Indian pupils. For Bangladeshi and Indian children, however, this variable had little effect. Except for West Indian pupils, time away from school was the major variable in the regression. School absence was for three reasons; illness, truancy or visiting the parents' country of origin. Clearly those who truant (perhaps the major reason for school absence) are also likely to perform poorly at school. This finding therefore, does not necessarily imply a cause and effect relationship whereby time away from school causes underachievement. This suggests that the process underlying educational achievement may be culture-dependent.

Social class has traditionally been associated with educational achievement in British society. This certainly is the case for the white children in the present sample (Table 7.8), but is true only for Pakistanis among the ethnic minority groups. The reason for this is not clear, but it may well be that recently migrated populations have not yet achieved social class levels which are commensurate with their aspirations and educational achievements. This is particularly likely to be true in a climate of structural discrimination against immigrants.

In the regression analyses (Tables 7.2 to 7.7) social class again failed to predict a significant amount of variance in the achievement in any ethnic group. In the case of the white pupils this was because although the effect of social class was initially significant, it failed to remain in the regression equation once the powerful effect of absence from school was controlled for.

Further evidence for the idea that educational achievement is culture-based was obtained from the 'median-split' analysis (Table 7.8).

In the whole sample, of the two most significant factors concerned with school – namely, school absence and enjoyment of school – neither is a true 'source factor' in that either may be interpreted in reverse; because children are achieving poorly at school they do not enjoy school and so play truant. The immediate environment provided three such source factors; the school, the peer group and the family. Parental interest and perceived parental and sibling help were the family elements, whilst the effects of 'social-self-peers' self-esteem, and perceived help (and hindrance) from other pupils were the peer-group element. The school element of the immediate environment was shown from the effects of 'school-academic' self-esteem, perceived help from teachers and from school. Social class was also a factor in the achievement process (though only for males) as in general self-esteem.

Although clearly evident, the differences between ethnic groups were complex. For example, self-esteem variables (except for those derived from interaction within the home) were important factors for white and West Indian pupils, but not for pupils of South Asian origin (Pakistanis, Bangladeshis and Indians). Conversely, paternal interest in school performance was important only for South Asian pupils. Moreover, only a single school-based source factor – perceived help from school – was involved in the achievement process for South Asian youngsters, but only so for Pakistani and not for either Indian or Bangladeshi adolescents. This tends to support Gupta's (1977) idea that parents are the major source of motivation for youngsters.

'General-self' self-esteem is involved in the achievement process for West Indian youngsters, and this tends to support Driver's (1980) interpretation of his findings for West Indian girls. It seems difficult to support Stone's (1981) idea, however, that self-esteem is unimportant in the achievement of West Indian adolescents.

These results, then, suggest that the process of examination achievement may be culture-dependent; factors affecting achievement in one ethnic group may not necessarily affect the achievement of another. It may be unwise therefore, to try to explain 'underachievement' in a particular ethnic minority group from an understanding of the achievement process of the majority group.

EDUCATIONAL MOTIVATION

So far we have shown that examination achievement is culture-based, implying that factors affecting the achievement of adolescents of certain ethnic groups do not necessarily affect achievement in other groups. Part of the achieving process concerns motivation; those with higher motivation tend to perform better. It was important, therefore, to assess whether any differences in the motivation to achieve existed between ethnic groups.

Two techniques were employed to determine this motivation; the first was a general test of 'achievement motivation' employing the Thematic Apperceptions Test (see Chapter Six for a description of the method). The second was the Motive–Attitude Intensity Scale devised by Sumner (1971).

For achievement motivation it was found that young people of South Asian origin tended to be motivated more by the 'fear of failure' aspect of achievement motivation than their white peers. Conversely, the white youngsters tended to be motivated more by the 'hope of success'. This difference suggests that South Asian youngsters wish to avoid the consequences of failure which may be either psychological (for example lower self-esteem) or socio-economic (for example having to perform jobs which prevent social mobility).

The findings from the Motive–Attitude Intensity Scale (Table 7.9) showed that those of South Asian origin had a significantly more positive attitude towards school and education than their white peers. A possible interpretation of this is that South Asian teenagers see formal education as a means of social and occupational mobility denied to their parents.

The research conducted in Phase Three also examined attitudes towards school and sources of motivation amongst fifteen-year-old pupils. It was confirmed that adolescents with immigrant origins have a higher regard for school than their indigenous counterparts. It was also found that white teenagers enjoy school significantly *less* than do the ethnic minority groups. The analysis of responses to the question 'how much do you enjoy school?' is presented in Table 7.10. The reasons for enjoying school were examined further during the semi-structured interviews (see Chapter Eight). Further analysis about how youngsters see the relationship between examination success and gaining employment related school enjoyment to the hope of social mobility. This relationship provided a link between two of the measures of educational achievement adopted in the present research – namely, examination achievement and entry into employment. A direct relationship has been questioned by Cuming (1983), but if such a relationship is seen as important by the young people then attempts to realise their vocational aspirations provide motivation for passing examinations. The results concerning their perceptions are set out in Table 7.11.

For the whole sample, over two-thirds believed that examination success leads to success in obtaining employment. The main exception to this trend was for West Indian youngsters, where only a small proportion saw a fairly strong relationship between passing examinations and gaining employment. A smaller group of South Asians (particularly Bangladeshis) also thought that the relationship was stronger than did the other groups.

The importance of examinations for South Asian youngsters is reflected in data relating to their intended response to examination failure. If failing examinations, the individuals in the sample had three choices: to retake them at school, to retake them at a college of further education, or not to retake them. One would expect that the greater the number intending to retake examinations, the more importance they place on them as a measure of achievement and future success. Moreover, the difference between those intending to retake at school and at college gives a rough idea of whether they were satisfied with the quality of school education. The proportion of the sample who intended to respond in each of these three ways is shown in Table 7.12. The results show that, again, the South Asian groups (particularly Pakistanis) emphasise examination success more than any other group. It is interesting that nearly half the white group intended to retake their examinations, if they failed, whilst more than two thirds of the South Asian sample intended to do so. The analysis shows that a large proportion of those intending to retake examinations wished to do so at school. The proportion who wanted to go to college, however, was non-uniform, with more West Indians and girls wishing to leave school. It is difficult to know if the generally low proportion of youngsters proposing to attend the local college (on examination failure) was because of ignorance about the function of a college of further education or a genuine preference for school.

An analysis of the interview data (see Chapter Eight) for those who had left school or had entered the sixth form clearly showed two types of teenagers failing their examinations. Those who had found work tended to minimise the role of examinations in the employment process; those who were unemployed tended to see examination failure as a main cause of occupational failure. There were some exceptions to this feature however; for example, an Indian boy who had returned to school to 'improve his exam results' believed he had not managed to get a job because he had been racially discriminated against. Not all those who intended to retake their examinations did so. Neither did all those who had not intended to retake actually leave school. Entry into the sixth form, as we outline in Chapter Eight, particularly for those with immigrant origins, was often the result of considerations other than academic achievement.

An aspect of the data which reinforces the idea that South Asian youngsters tend to put greater faith than other groups in education as a means of social mobility concerned the intentions of the school-leavers. Such intentions fell into four main categories (Table 7.13): getting a job; higher education (tertiary college, college of higher education, schools of nursing etc); others (including 'getting married' and 'being unemployed'). Intentions on leaving school differed significantly across ethnic and sexual groups.

There appeared, then, to be a number of differences between the ethnic groups studied in terms of educational motivation: the motivation of South Asian young people in particular appeared centred around a commitment to school and examination success, possibly in the hope of social mobility, or, more likely, to avoid the damaging effect of failure.

Despite the greater commitment to education among South Asian youngsters, this cannot explain their relatively high achievement levels compared to other groups, as school-based variables were unimportant factors in the achieving process of those teenagers. This was not so for either white or West Indian youngsters, where a lack of commitment to education, and so a reduction in motivation to perform well at school, tended to lead to low achievement.

Motivation to achieve well in examinations (one of the measures of educational achievement adopted here) also appeared to be related to hopes of future employment. It should be noted that in obtaining work the adolescents (regardless of ethnic origin) had a somewhat unrealistic view of life after school. Eighty-three per cent of them believed they would get the job they wanted on leaving school, and only six per cent of the sample indicated that they expected to obtain employment other than their first choice. Although it appeared that the pupils themselves believed their aspirations were realistic, the projected level of unemployment for them on leaving school was 74 per cent (Bradford MDC, 1982).

EDUCATIONAL ACHIEVEMENT: THE IMMEDIATE ENVIRONMENT

The relative influence of the three constituents of the immediate environment (the school, the family and the peer group) were analysed in terms of sources of help and hindrance in passing examinations. Each element of the immediate environment was represented by two possible responses, whilst a seventh response of 'others' was included to ensure an open set of options. The proportion of responses for each source is given in Tables 7.14 and 7.15.

The Influence of the School

In terms of help in passing examinations, then, the youngsters rated 'school' sources with almost equal potency. The influence of the peer group in helping pupils to pass examinations is much more restricted, with only about a sixth indicating help from one or other of the peer group response-options. There were no significant differences between either ethnic or sex grouping, except for help obtained from school. This was rated very high by Indians and rated low by the West Indians.

Interpretation of this result must consider the factors relating to achievement – outlined earlier – for each ethnic group. Indian teenagers tend to think school helps them to pass examinations, but this is not important in understanding the process of achievement for them. It is interesting, however, in relation to the trend of South Asian youngsters to rate school highly. This is because perceived help from school was not a factor discriminating between high and low achieving Indian youngsters. The reverse is true for West Indian youngsters; perceived help from school was important in separating high and low achieving pupils. Only a few of them (11 per cent) thought school was helpful in passing examinations and this is important when considering their educational achievement.

The Influence of the Family

The family forms the second element of the immediate environment. Much information about the influence of the family was obtained in the form of semi-structured interviews. Nevertheless, throughout the research a number of questions about the influence of parents and other family members were covered within the various questionnaires and tests.

The pupils were asked to indicate the degree of interest they thought their parents took in them and their future career, and the findings showed that for *all* ethnic groups perceived maternal influence was greater than perceived paternal influence in formulating future aspirations. On the whole, too, there was little difference between white and South Asian youngsters in their perceptions of parental interest. The data also indicated a marked 'ceiling effect', that is, a large proportion of both white and South Asian respondents revealed a tendency to choose the highest point on the scale (a great interest). There was only one significant inter-ethnic difference: high maternal and low paternal interest were characteristic of West Indian youngsters, whilst for all other ethnic groups the two perceived levels of interest were more equally rated. No significant differences were found between the ethnic groups in terms of perceived parental interest. The 'ceiling effect' was much reduced, however, with less than half of the teenagers opting for the highest point on the scale concerning paternal interest, and 58 per cent for maternal interest. The findings for perceived parental interest are shown in Tables 7.16 and 7.17.

Despite the apparent reduction in perceived parental interest (which probably occurred by changing from a four to a five point scale, introduced to try to reduce the 'ceiling effect'), perceived maternal interest was more pronounced than paternal interest. It is interesting that in the case of white, Pakistani and West Indian youngsters, maternal interest seemed to be a major determinant of high and low achievement in examination success, whereas for the South Asian youngsters paternal interest was apparently a major determinant. A close examination of the data revealed that the difference between perceived maternal and paternal interest was one determinant of achievement. It is quite likely that these patterns emerged from the outcome of the different family structures of the cultural groups. South Asian families, for example, are characteristically patriarchal, West Indian families matriarchal and white families a mixture of the two (though more often patriarchal).

In this research the role of brothers and sisters in examination performance was also considered; were they a help or a hindrance to the youngsters? More than two to one thought they were helpful and (as earlier with the perceived sources of help in passing) sex and ethnicity were significant in the responses. Compared to Pakistanis who cited siblings least as a source of hindrance, West Indians thought they were a most frequent source of difficulty. This may reflect differing family styles in their cultures, but it made no difference to the group achievement.

Maternal influence was also evident in the formation of educational aspirations (i.e. what the youngster wished to do on leaving school). In the first and third phases of the research, pupils were asked what jobs they wished to do on leaving full-time education. They were also asked to indicate the jobs their fathers (paternal aspiration) would wish them to seek on completing their education. The data derived from the two stages were remarkably similar, showing the mother to be a predominant influence in aspiration formation. The correlational analysis between the pupil's own aspiration and those of his or her parents were computed according to ethnic group and sex (Table 7.18).

From the data we can see that, except for Bangladeshi youngsters, fathers' aspirations did not really correspond with the youngsters' own vocational aspirations, whereas the mothers' did. The correspondence for the latter was greater if there were migrant origins. To some extent this supports Gupta's (1977) hypothesis about maternal influence on South Asian adolescents' vocational aspirations.

There were also highly significant differences across ethnic groups concerning the social class of the job desired by the adolescents before leaving school. Those of South Asian origin tended to aspire to more upward social mobility than either white or West Indian youngsters. Why this should be so is impossible to say from this study.

The relative influence of the family in the achievement process, particularly when related to entry into employment, may be seen from two aspects of the data: sources of information concerning employment and help in gaining employment.

Sources of information about various occupations have an important part to play in the aspiration formation process because the information an individual receives may determine his/her attitudes towards certain occupations. It is common for the school to provide some form of careers education where information about jobs is imparted, and this may be conducted either by teachers within the school, careers officers from the local authority, or both. As well as these formal sources, the pupils may also acquire information about jobs from members of family, friends and the media. The percentage of young people who acknowledged receiving support from each source is presented in Table 7.19.

The results reveal a subtle difference in the sources of information across ethnic groups. The major source of information for the white population was the family (70 per cent); for those with immigrant origins, however, this role was adopted by the school and the Careers

Office. Moreover, whereas the white group placed 'friends' ahead of 'careers officers' this was not the case for the ethnic minority pupils.

The Influence of the Peer Group

Seventy per cent of teenagers thought other pupils influenced their academic performance. The peer group was the principal source of hindrance in passing examinations. This may reflect streaming in school where, perhaps, less disruption was tolerated in higher streams.

SELF-ESTEEM AND THE IMMEDIATE ENVIRONMENT

Analysis of the factors linked to achievement revealed that for the white and West Indian groups the elements of self-esteem were important within the achievement process. The Coopersmith Self-Esteem Inventory (SEI), used throughout the research, yielded measures of self-esteem derived from interactions at home, at school and with the peer group, in addition to the general-self component. It was possible, therefore, to assess the proportion of self-esteem derived from each source. Because of the nature of the SEI the comparison criteria of each source are as follows: 50 per cent general-self; 17 per cent school-academic; 17 per cent social-self-peers; 17 per cent home-parents. The percentages for each source are shown according to ethnicity and sex in Table 7.22.

This analysis revealed the relative importance of each element of the immediate environment for each cultural group. For West Indian youngsters the peer group seemed a major contributor to self-esteem, whilst interactions within the school were of lesser importance. On the whole, South Asian youngsters (particularly Bangladeshi and Indian) derived a greater part of their self-esteem from interactions at school than either of the other two groups, whilst interactions within the home were very important for Bangladeshi adolescents.

Analysis of Variance was also conducted on the scores obtained on each of the Coopersmith Self-Esteem Inventory sub-scales. No statistically significant differences emerged concerning the ethnic groups studied, and this implies that the level of self-esteem is unaffected by the individual's ethnicity. A significant sex difference did emerge, however, on the 'general self' component where females had significantly higher self-esteem than males (Tables 7.21 and 7.22).

Analysis of self-esteem data obtained within the first stage showed that South Asian youngsters had higher total self-esteem than their white counterparts and this was significantly related to vocational aspirations; the highest correlations were obtained for the 'school-academic' element of self-esteem. In a follow-up study of these youngsters after leaving school, however, (phase two of the research) this situation was reversed. Self-esteem levels, moreover, were affected by their employment status and whether they had achieved their job aspirations (Tables 7.21 and 7.22).

Status after reaching the statutory school-leaving age was divided into three categories; those who had left school and obtained work; those who had left school but were unemployed; those who had entered the sixth form. Analysis of Variance assessed the effects of status on self-esteem; the effects of ethnicity and gender were also included. The results of these analyses are shown in Tables 7.23 to 7.26.

Although the direct effects of sex, status and ethnicity did not reach any acceptable level of statistical significance, the interactions between the three factors need attention. The 'sex × status' interaction arose because unemployment had more effect on male self-esteem than on female. The 'sex × ethnic group' interaction arose because the general self-esteem of South Asians (Pakistanis in particular) was lower than that of white and West Indian girls; the reverse was true for the boys. The 'status × ethnic group' interaction may have arisen because unemployment had more impact on the general self-esteem of the South Asian youths than on the white or West Indian youngsters. The three-way interaction was a complex combination in which the self-esteem of the various sub-groups was differently affected.

The school-academic component of self-esteem operated differently. Here the direct effects of status and ethnicity were significant. The former arose because the school-academic self-esteem of sixth formers was significantly higher than for those who had left school. The effect of ethnic group arose because the self-esteem of Indians and Pakistanis was higher than those of other ethnic groups (see Table 7.23).

The effect of status on social-self-peers' self-esteem occurred because the self-esteem of the unemployed was lower than that of those in work or those who had stayed on at school in the sixth form. The 'sex × ethnic group' interaction occurred because the social-self-peers self-esteem of South Asian girls was lower than that for white and West Indian girls, though this was untrue for boys (Table 7.24).

Unlike other aspects of self-esteem, the variables of sex, status or ethnic group had no significant effect on self-esteem derived from the home. This may be because almost all the youngsters were still living with parents. It is less likely, therefore, that the individual's status would affect self-esteem from this source (Table 7.25).

Clearly, status appears to have had a strong effect on the total self-esteem of adolescents. Although levels of self-esteem were similar for those employed and those in the sixth form, those who had left school and were unemployed had significantly lower self-esteem. Again the interactional effects are noteworthy, even though none reached statistical significance at the 5 per cent level. The composite self-esteem performed similarly to the 'general-self' component (which is 50 per cent of composite self-esteem on the Coopersmith scale). The effects here then, are mainly the result of fluctuations in the 'general-self' component reported earlier (Table 7.26).

Three important points about self-esteem emerged from the analysis of the data: white adolescents had higher self-esteem than the South Asians; those in employment had significantly higher self-esteem than the jobless; youngsters who had exceeded their expectations for jobs had higher self-esteem than those not achieving them. In all these findings neither sex differences nor interactions were significant.

THE END OF COMPULSORY SCHOOLING

The lower self-esteem of the South Asians in this particular sample can be partly attributed to the effects of unemployment and failure to achieve aspirations. Analysis of the Phase Two data showed that unemployment was higher for South Asian youngsters on leaving school (43 per cent) than for white youngsters (27 per cent). Moreover, of those who had managed to obtain work, the standard of that work for South Asian adolescents was significantly lower than that of the white group. This aspect was assessed by the KOSS classification system (see Dept. of Employment *Gazette*, 1972). This 'underemployment' might have led to more South Asian teenagers failing to attain their aspirations (79 per cent) than the white ones (51 per cent).

Why would obtaining a job be difficult? What did the sample think would be the reasons? Here a significant ethnic-group difference existed. Those of South Asian origin (particularly Pakistanis) tended to mention 'internal' reasons, whereas white and West Indian youngsters tended to state 'external' ones. South Asian youngsters, therefore, believed they would find difficulty in getting jobs because they did not have the appropriate attributes (examination success, etc.), whereas the white and West Indian youngsters tended to blame difficulties on the 'depressed' labour market in West Yorkshire.

When the teenagers were asked who would be at fault if they failed to obtain work on leaving school 65 per cent felt they would be to blame; 54 per cent blamed the government; 12 per cent blamed the employers; 5 per cent thought teachers were to blame; 4 per cent blamed friends, and 1 per cent said parents. This suggests that the largest part of the sample took personal responsibility for finding employment. This high percentage explains some of the reduction in self-esteem experienced by unemployed school-leavers.

These findings only apply to those who had left school, and the result was moderated by examining the ethnic constitution of those who had stayed on into the sixth form. There was a disproportionate number of South Asian youngsters who had decided to remain at school; only 9 per cent of the white group was in full-time education compared to 41 per cent of the South Asian group. This suggests that the different groups employ different strategies for deciding when to leave school. Whereas the white group would leave school as early as possible and then search for work, the South Asian youngsters tended to stay on at school as long as possible. More than two-thirds of the white pupils intended to leave school to seek employment, whereas in the South Asian and West Indian groups only about one-third intended to do so. One of the outcomes of this difference in strategies was that the academic qualifications of the white group who left school at sixteen were higher than those of the corresponding South Asian and West Indian groups. Those South Asians most likely to achieve tended to remain in full-time education. There were no significant differences between ethnic groups concerning the recency of vocational decisions. Girls, however, tended to decide what they wished to do on leaving school earlier than boys.

The pupils were also asked to indicate which factors they thought helpful in gaining employment. The list of factors was devised to include: personal ones, (being clever, being nice); formal sources (good careers advice, good school record); informal sources (knowing the 'right' people). The number and proportion of teenagers who responded positively to each source category are shown according to ethnicity and sex in Table 7.20.

Except for West Indian pupils, who tended to rate a good school record as an important source of help in getting a job (although they felt that passing examinations was relatively unimportant), parental advice was seen as the most important source of help. This shows the relative influence parents have in the choices made by adolescents.

A further interesting trend in the data concerned the relative importance of 'knowing the right people'. This was rated as helpful in gaining employment by 43 per cent of the white sample; the response rate for the ethnic minority groups, however, was much lower (e.g. 20 per cent for Pakistanis); there was a significant sex difference, with males believing that 'knowing the right people' was more important than did the females.

The family, particularly parents, appeared to be a major source of influence for all youngsters, but did not perform the same role for each ethnic group. Maternal concern was more important for white and West Indian groups, for example, but paternal concern was more important for young people of South Asian origin. Moreover, in making choices which would affect the pupil after leaving school (as in aspiration formation) the home became the major influence for all the youngsters.

SUMMARY

Given the intricacies of the quantitative findings it was felt necessary to summarise them:

Factors discriminating between 'high' and 'low' examination achievement were dissimilar for each ethnic group:

(i)   *For white adolescents*, the main factors were:
      level of self-esteem, including general-self, peer-group and
          school-academic dimensions
      social class
      perceived level of maternal interest
      perceived level of help from the following sources: teachers,
          school, parents, siblings and friends
      enjoyment of school
      school-attendance/absence

(ii) *For Pakistani adolescents*, the main factors were:
      use of mother tongue at home
      social class
      perceived level of paternal *and* maternal interest

perceived level of help from: school and siblings
enjoyment of school
school attendance/absence

(iii) *For Bangladeshi adolescents*, the main factors were:
perceived level of paternal interest
school attendance/absence

(iv) *For Indian adolescents*, the main factors were:
perccived level of paternal interest
enjoyment of school
school attendance/absence

(v) *For West Indian adolescents*, the main factors were:
level of self-esteem, including its general-self and school-
academic dimensions
perceived level of maternal interest
perceived level of help from school
school attendance/absence

The above factors, although found to discriminate between high and low achievement, represent only part of a complex interaction which is different for each ethnic group. Other factors, despite not reaching statistical significance, also mediated on each interaction complex, making each unique. Thus, school attendance/absence, a discriminating factor in *all* ethnic groups, has a separate value for *each* group. It cannot therefore be considered as having equal value in characterising high and low achievement in all ethnic groups.

In motivation to achieve, *self-esteem* was important for whites and West Indians, *parental interest* in school performance for South Asians in general, and *perceived school help* for Pakistanis.

Most teenagers emphasised *examination success*; this was of greater importance to the South Asian group than for any other single ethnic group. The South Asians were more positive to and enjoyed school more; in this they may have been motivated by the hope for later social or occupational upward mobility or even by 'fear of failure'. Among the whites, high achievers appeared to be motivated by 'hope of success'; those showing a lack of commitment to school tended to be among the low achievers. Those teenagers unsuccessful in finding employment maximised the importance of examinations in the achievement process; those finding employment minimised their importance.

Perceived *paternal*, rather than *maternal interest* was greater for the South Asian groups; with the exception of the Bangladeshi youngsters, *fathers' job aspirations for their children* did not correspond to those of the youngsters themselves; *mothers' job aspirations for their children* showed greater correspondence particularly in the ethnic minority groups. Perceived *maternal interest* was greater for West Indian youngsters. Those differences may reflect differing family structures in the ethnic groups. Parental advice about jobs was considered important by all youngsters.

Although some were subsequently unfulfilled, *post-16 intentions* differed significantly across ethnic and sex groups. All groups showed a low degree of realism in *job aspirations* and the home played a major part in their formation. Almost five times more South Asians than whites continued their education beyond 16; many who did stayed on in school as long as possible. White school-leavers at 16 tended to have higher qualifications than their ethnic minority counterparts.

For South Asian youngsters generally, *school interactions* were an important source of self-esteem, although for Bangladeshis *home interactions* were most important. The *peer group* was the most important source of *self-esteem* for West Indians. All youngsters finding employment had higher *self-esteem* than the jobless ones, as had those who exceeded their employment expectations relative to those who failed them. South Asian girls tended to have lower levels of *self-esteem* than boys. The reverse was the case in the white and West Indian groups.

Failure to meet job aspirations was higher among South Asian school-leavers than among whites. South Asians tended to 'internalise' the reasons for their lack of success; their white and West Indian counterparts tended to 'externalise' those reasons. *Knowing the right people* was considered important in terms of finding a job among almost half the white youngsters; in the ethnic minority groups this figure did not exceed one-fifth.

8 Educational Achievement: Perceptions and Attitudes

When looking at the influences on achievement we must remember that conclusions drawn from statistical evidence are only one side of the coin. Such conclusions may offer people scant comfort. The perceptions of individuals add the human dimension to the statistical argument. Whilst those perceptions are harder to quantify – they cannot be added up and set out neatly in tabular form – they provide a reminder of the expectations held of education by individuals and of the realities with which the individual wrestles to comprehend his or her world. In this chapter we will consider these realities.

During this research many tape-recorded interviews were conducted. These sought to pursue issues arising from the research in a way offering a more flexible response than that allowed by the use of questionnaires (Verma and Beard, 1981). Interview data were considered complementary to the data derived from questionnaires and tests.

The interviews were conducted mostly in the homes of the young people, though occasionally on school premises or in university offices, when this was more convenient for the interviewee.

The interviews were only semi-structured; this meant that although a limited range of issues was to be discussed, the interviewee was not confined to a prescriptive sequence of questions. In this way the questions were to offer the person free expression of his/her views and experiences within the framework of issues considered fundamental to the research. The interviewers sought to make the interviews as near to 'actual conversations' as possible.

Analysis and presentation of transcribed interview data cause more problems than the tabulation of figures from questionnaire data; the latter's results may be presented with minimal interpretation, even though this may be subjective in its selectivity, (Willis, 1977). The major problem with using interview data is that, by their nature, interviews allow many possible responses to any given question. Attempts at analysis and interpretation of responses inevitably result in the views and experiences of the interviewees being mediated by the researcher's perception.

In presenting the interview findings we have attempted to strike a balance between the general and the particular. The general seeks to reflect prevalent attitudes, opinions and experiences amongst those interviewed, whilst the particular seeks to reflect individual stand-points which were considered either to typify the views of a group or sex or to offer a novel perspective on the issues being discussed.

Inevitably such a process is an arbitrary one and so the individual's comments about an issue may not fully reflect his or her overall thought-processes. Nevertheless, the insights gained from interview data complement those from analysis of questionnaire and test results. As a result a more rounded picture of the situation emerges as the strengths of each approach are combined and the weaknesses of each are minimised.

EDUCATIONAL ACHIEVEMENT AND THE IMMEDIATE ENVIRONMENT

The Influence of the School

It was mentioned earlier that school was a major influence on pupil achievement and the data presented here seem to confirm this. Combined with other influences the pupil's perceptions of school show the varied strands comprising the total picture.

Analysis suggested that those of South Asian origin had a more 'positive' attitude to school than either white or West Indian youngsters; from a comparison of answers of South Asian pupils (Pakistani, Bangladeshi and Indian) with those of white pupils, two things emerged. Firstly, the former, generally had less to say. Secondly, they usually gave overall approval to school, school work and teaching whereas the latter tended to be more selective in their likes and dislikes and offered more judgement on schools and teachers.

About half the South Asians commented that they enjoyed or liked school. Of these, one was sometimes bored, another was given too much homework (four subjects per night) but felt lost without any, whilst another would like to attend school seven days a week; only one admitted finding English difficult. A pupil claimed that he gave the impression that he disliked school although he really liked it. Two who disliked school found the rules restrictive and considered that there was insufficient independence. A girl disliked school although she enjoyed school work; perhaps she found social relations difficult, for when she was the only girl to attend draughtsman classes, the boys were 'rude'. A boy in a CSE stream hated all teachers except for one; he enjoyed an electrical link course and wished that his school ran more courses like that. One pupil disapproved of 'idle disruptive pupils', whilst another thought his head teacher did nothing for pupils', unlike some other teachers he knew.

In contrast, white pupils tended to name subjects they liked and sometimes those they did not like: maths, physics, chemistry and geography were enjoyed by a boy who thought that school was poor preparation for working life. A girl who thought her school had helped her only in English and maths found lessons boring as she was not offered the typing option she had requested. One boy who liked school, especially craft and games, felt that some children should be controlled more, for one or two teachers did not care. He added, however, that the English teacher had been a great help to him; he considered, too, that school choices could be limiting. A girl said that school was all right, but could not think of anything it had done for her. A boy who liked technology and maths, but not metal-work or science, thought school had been a little help, but not a lot. He found teachers quite strict but added that they varied with discipline. A girl taking GCE 'O' levels complained that the work for the 'O' level did not begin until the fourth year. She thought that more should be expected of pupils from the beginning. A boy who regularly truanted in the fifth year to help a milkman did so because he found lessons boring.

Less than half the interviewees offered views on what was important at school. Only those of South Asian origin mentioned the importance of learning about manners and how to interact socially. The remaining comments, like those of white pupils, referred to having an education, getting qualifications and being helped to find or prepare for work.

Exceptional comments came from a white boy and a boy whose parents were European. The first said that he was halfway through the fifth form before realising that working at school mattered and he regretted this. He thought the most important thing at school was 'your mates, having a laugh and a joke'. The other considered that big schools were not useful in our society; he would like smaller schools emphasising vocational teaching, 'having stricter discipline, a uniform, more exercise, less science subjects and political teaching', and said that this should continue to the age of 18.

The interviewees who entered the sixth form generally had a more positive attitude towards school. The comments made by white pupils about the school in general tended to concentrate on comparisons between life in the fifth and sixth forms. Emphasis was placed on the pressures of work, revision and completion of homework: 'We were drilled and drilled to get revising' said one. Other remarks from the successful white pupils questioned the wisdom of an 'open' sixth form. One pupil believed there should be a minimum number of 'O' level passes required before one could take 'A' levels: 'I think a lot have stayed on when they are not really capable of doing "A" levels.'

In general, the South Asian sixth-formers made very positive and extremely favourable comments about the school and their education. Blame was not aimed at school, even when they were unsuccessful in getting work at the end of the fifth form and so stayed on into the sixth form. They genuinely appeared to enjoy friendships they had made and to miss these during school holidays.

The attitude of fifth-form school-leavers tended to express more grievances about their education than those who had stayed on into the sixth form. Some pupils blamed inadequate teaching and, thereby, teachers: one said:

> Teachers didn't care much, kids do anything and that so on the last day when we had to leave school we were really glad to leave that school 'cos we didn't like it much.

Sometimes pupils felt that teachers disliked them and it was difficult, therefore, to behave naturally with them. A Pakistani girl said:

> You try to humour them [teachers] . . . they treat you as though you are from another planet or something. If you get on well with them they stop hating you . . . but you have got to try first. If you start putting a barrier between them and you, they hate you more, so you have always got to try to be on your best side for them.

But there were also felt to be racially prejudiced teachers: a Sikh boy commented '. . . because I am Indian, that is a disadvantage. Some teachers have very poor expectations of all Asians', whilst another said 'the teacher didn't get on well with me neither 'cos I was Asian and we only had about two or three Asians in our group, she always picked on us or something'.

Such prejudice was also found in the young people's peer group at certain schools. An Indian girl compared her earlier school experiences with her present ones, saying:

When I was in junior school I never bothered about my colour . . . since I have come to this school I have encountered a lot of racial prejudice and I realised that I was this colour, and it was this colour that was making them so horrible to me.

A Tanzanian girl was made to feel uncomfortable too. She said:

Well, some people, that's what I don' like, some people are really against you, racialist mostly here [at this school] . . . and it's just that I don't like it. It's just like people's attitudes . . . Being Indian, I think this is a disadvantage.

The peer group could also cause problems for white pupils. Some blamed it for their poor academic performance: 'a quarter of it was probably my own fault anyway – I mean, I got in with the wrong crowd when I first started here'. This white girl attributed the other three-quarters to the poor discipline in the school.

Despite these criticisms, approximately half of those who left school were pleased with the quality of the education they had received. Those who were satisfied, however, tended to be less vocal than those who were not.

Those who held the school responsible, at least in part, for poor achievement, gave varied reasons for this. 'There were so many different teachers' said a white girl, 'you thought, have I got a chance of passing this exam? and you would look back on what had happened in years gone by and you couldn't judge, because you had had so many different teachers. I think that is what happened in maths, I failed that 'cos I had too many teachers'. Another Indian boy commented on both inadequate teaching and lack of facilities for 'A' level study.

There were wide variations in how schools prepared pupils for leaving. Only a small minority from one school had experience of mock interviewing or form filling, but those who did felt it was useful.

Views about careers education varied. Some felt it had been a hindrance:

> Well there was a careers teacher at school and we used to go and see her about once a week. But every kind of job we said we wanted, she would try and put us off. (White girl)

> We had careers lessons in with the general education lessons but I don't know she seemed to have her own ideas and if she did not think you were suitable for the job she would disillusion you on what you wanted to do – she would say well I don't think that is really for you and if you had your heart set on it – if she thought you weren't too clever for the job – like hairdressing – she told me I was far too clever to do hairdressing – I don't know she seemed to have her own ideas. If she didn't want you to be what you wanted to be she would put you off. 'Cos I mentioned the police force and she obviously didn't like the police force so she tried to put me off but nobody could do that because I am influenced from home you see. (White girl)

Some were indifferent to careers education, believing it to be a waste of time and money:

> Yes, there was a weekly careers. They had a careers teacher there and you have a careers interview. I don't honestly know how often it was, I can't remember. But to be quite honest, I thought they were a waste of money, they were no help at all – I suppose to others they may be, but to me they weren't. (White boy)

> Nobody really bothered about the careers teacher, to be quite honest. Because what she said was a load of codswallop anyway. (South Asian boy)

At times careers teachers appeared to try to persuade people to adopt unwanted or even inappropriate careers. A Pakistani boy said:

> The careers teachers were trying to get me into engineering and forcing me, and they were saying don't stay on at school, it's bad for you. You will never make 'A' levels and discouraged like hell they did. You really got put off and the only thing that keeps you going is your friends who say 'don't listen to them, you'll do all right'.

Another Pakistani boy commented:

> The careers officers asked me why I don't want to take up
> agriculture as my career. He said that my father comes from a rural
> area of Pakistan.

But some saw careers education as a help:

> Oh yes, we had a few lessons a week on careers and everything you
> know and we had a careers officer who came in once or twice a week,
> who we could go and visit in our lunch hour or on an evening. It was
> very helpful if you wanted to go deeper into a career or anything.
> She would give you all the information, plus we had a common room
> where we had various information on careers.   (South Asian girl)

> No, he didn't discourage me. He told me that there were various
> kinds of job for a chartered accountant, and all that, and said he
> would send me leaflets, which he did.   (South Asian boy)

Although this variation in views is partly because several schools were
involved in the research, the pupils' expectations were also
responsible. One white girl said 90 per cent of the girls in her school
had already decided what they wanted to do on leaving and so required
no advice. She felt that this made it difficult for teachers to interest
them.

Of those who acknowledged needing help the majority were
satisfied with the extent and quality of careers advice. Some pupils,
both ethnic minorities and white, found films about jobs 'informative
and interesting'. A number had favourable comments to make about
work experience: 'I went on work experience in the fifth form to
Thornton View Hospital and I really enjoyed it with the old people,
and then I went to a nursery – you know another aspect of nursing –
and I really enjoyed that as well so I thought that is what I will do.'
Although the opportunity to partake in work experience was available
to all pupils in one school, not all were interested. Some believed it was
more suitable for the less able ones and it would also mean missing
valuable school time in the fifth form. 'It was for kind of lower jobs you
know, I didn't want to do anything like that' said one pupil. Moreover,
some pupils were critical of their advisers: 'The careers teacher doesn't
tell you what you need – only where to get a leaflet' was one comment.

Generally, formal lessons and courses about careers, if mentioned, were not praised. A South Asian boy commented that he had had six lessons a week, but these were not interesting; they did not include what he wanted to do or anything that would interest him. A white pupil commented that careers teaching was not very good, people just came in from firms to talk.

The school, then, is a major influence on the achievement of youngsters, both in terms of passing examinations and looking for employment. The nature and extent of this influence, however, depends largely on the other characteristics of the individual.

The influence of the school would be incomplete if it were to be confined to illustrations of pupils' perceptions. Therefore, extracts from interviews with teachers are presented to illustrate the type of stereotyping of ethnic minority pupils which some teachers engage in, either consciously of unconsciously. Such stereotyping is likely to adversely effect teachers' interactions with pupils, with many attendant consequences for the latter's educational achievement, and ultimately, life-chances.

There is a certain tendency amongst some of them [Asians], to believe that knowledge and ability can be boxed and taken down from a shelf, and the ingredients of that box can be put in front of them and all that they need to do is to soak it up, recharge themselves like a battery with academic standing; that's very sad because there's a great tendency to believe among the Asian community – to think sheer diligence is sufficient, and it is not.

(Teacher)

They [Asians] approach their ambitions with the hopes of obtaining a particular post or particular places, and yet academically they are not bright enough, so that they set their aims too high, and although a school will try very often to indicate this to them, they don't really want to know and therefore they switch off.   (Teacher)

We have no distinction in this school between pupil and pupil, that's our first objective . . . I should have put it – if all the Asians . . . evaporated tomorrow, it would not make a scrap of difference to the curriculum.   (Teacher)

. . . the people [Asians] you are talking about, their sons and daughters finish up in this school in classes which are non-examinations or bottom CSE. They rarely have sons and daughters

who are going to be bright GCE candidates, and it isn't the fault of
the education system, and it isn't the fault of Western civilisation –
it's inherent in life.   (Teacher)

The Influence of the Family

Family influences, particularly parents, were mentioned more
frequently than any other. Almost without exception these were seen
as being positive by providing specific advice, by general support or by
motivation. There seemed to be two differences across the ethnic
groups. Firstly, West Indians tended to mention their mother more
frequently than their father, and secondly the South Asian parents
tended to give more advice or direct guidance. A few comments will
show this:

> I think it's the ones who have got parents that insist on getting a good
> job. If you have parents that are not really bothered about your
> schooling, then you'll not get on.   (White boy)

> Well it is just a matter of having a lot of ambition and having that will
> to go forward. 'Cos I don't intend to just stay where I am. I want to
> go forward in life 'cos that is how I have been brought up. Well I
> think I have been carried through by my parents; through what I
> have seen them do and the amount of work they have put into life to
> get where they are now. They started in a one room flat and they've
> come up to this. [a well appointed semi-detached house]. So that is a
> lot of motivation. I would like to excel even more than what they
> have done.   (West Indian boy)

> To do well you need a good relationship with your parents – good
> relationships with the family as a whole. I think if you have got your
> parents and the family you can face anything in the world. That's my
> belief.   (Indian girl)

> My mum was always very eager, she was always pushing me and
> stuff, so I didn't want to let my mum down and my family down. So I
> just got down to it really. But you couldn't go out or anything. So I
> just saw a lot of other girls and they were going out with boy-friends
> and all this, but in the end they only ended up with two or three ['O'
> levels] and like the Headmaster would say, they will just end up as
> underachievers.   (West Indian girl)

Other comments included that of a white girl who said that her mother was 'more like a big sister really'.

A number of the Asian young people said that their parents had migrated in order to provide them with a good education:

> The only reason anyone comes here is that education is better, it's free and in Pakistan pupils have to cross rivers and walk miles a day. Here there is the luxury of buses. So we come here for education so we can go home and say we have got a qualification and get a job and settle down and that's it. That's the whole point in coming here I think. (Pakistani boy)

In fairness, such statements about returning to the country of origin were quite rare. The emphasis placed by parents on education, however, placed considerable pressure on their children to do well. A Pakistani boy said:

> Asian parents are really looking towards a good future for their sons, they are the base of the family. Actually the girls do the housework, but it would help if they are educated, but they don't rely as much on them as they do on sons.

Other, similar interviews included the case of an Indian girl whose parents wanted her to become a doctor; her father always told her to get a good education and so she decided to become a nursery nurse. An Asian boy who wanted to be a pilot received support for this by his parents although he was doubtful of obtaining the necessary qualifications. Another boy going to a College of Further Education to take five 'O' levels wanted to get 'A' levels to proceed to University. A boy taking five 'O' levels thought his parents would not like him to work in textiles after this study.

Some Asian youngsters had mentioned close relations who held posts requiring higher education. In such families parents seemed particularly anxious that their sons should do well in the world and that daughters should be well qualified. Indian parents who owned a number of small shops wished their daughter to have a technical or scientific career. An Indian boy who came to England from Australia at the age of seven was going into the sixth form and wanted to go to University perhaps to study Management or Surveying; his brothers and sisters had already shown considerable achievement. Another boy, with very able relatives, was taking 'A' levels to obtain a job using sciences, preferably medicine, but he acknowledged that this would require much hard work.

The Influence of the Peer Group

A characteristic of the individual (mentioned earlier on page 105) concerns the peer group influence. By 'peer group', of course, we mean other pupils in school and the youngsters' friends outside. The way the peer group affected young people was important too.

This group's influence also was very varied. For some they were a help in passing examinations:

> You need someone to sort of let the lid off. I go to my friends say for an hour after school just to get out of it for a bit. And there it is, you have got your friends egging you on – have you done that homework, have you done this?   (West Indian girl)

For others they were seen as a primary source of information about jobs. 'My friend brought some college leaflets over, and he said that it will be better for you, so I discussed it with my parents', said a white boy. The peer group was even a source of pressure; one Indian girl regretted going to college:

> I went to college probably because most of the other children were leaving as well and they were going to college. And you felt odd if you stayed on at school when your friends were leaving and going to college. Well, after I went to college I thought that I should have stayed on really.

Analysis of the data showed that most pupils commented similarly about the effect of the peer group on achievement.

A particularly interesting pattern to emerge from the interviews was the imbalance in intercultural understanding. Although all those interviewed had spent considerable time in multi-ethnic schools the South Asian pupils had adopted a number of English cultural values, but the indigenous population had failed to understand the position of the other ethnic groups. One Indian girl expressed this as follows:

> When I look at English friends and I look at them sometimes, and I think I wouldn't do that because my Indian upbringing has taught

me not to do some things. We can understand them because we have lived here all the time but they find it difficult to understand us, they don't know what it is based on at all. I explain some things to my friends but they just don't understand.

English youngsters expect cultural pluralism to work in one direction, that is immigrants should adopt the values of the indigenous culture, and this is clear from the comments of one English girl:

Obviously Asians don't get as far as we do because of their families and religions – especially the girls – the girls marry at an early age, their parents say to them that you should get married and have a family and stay at home. You don't see many Asian women at work, as you do English. You tend to see them more with children and just staying at home. I think some of them, that have got used to the English culture, I think they must have felt a lot of resentment.

There can be little doubt that South Asian teenagers had been affected by living in England. Although many interviewees found it difficult to express the feelings arising from being 'caught between two cultures', it was clear that some Asian young people felt somewhat confused about their cultural identity:

I am proud of being English, but I am more proud of being Indian. I don't agree with my Mum and Dad hardly ever, but if it comes to the crunch I am more Indian than I am English. I think my own kids will be very Western but they will never forget their own culture.

(Indian boy)

Clearly he felt that his own children would be less 'Indian' than himself, but by the phrase 'their own culture', he was referring to Indian rather than Western values. This boy was in some difficulty in deciding what was right. His parents were devout Sikhs, and, despite having rejected much of the faith himself, he did not want to bring disgrace upon his parents:

Well the only reason he [his father] came over was to get a better education for his children. I don't want to let my father down – his sole ambition was to come over here and educate his children because the education in India is non-existent.

Nevertheless, in secret he had been going out with an English girlfriend whose parents were openly racially prejudiced. He expressed his relief that he could talk to someone who 'understood' (that is, the interviewer) but who would not tell anyone, and it is thought that the research interview was the first time he had been able to discuss his situation. To some extent he had been able to resolve some of the cultural conflicts – at least to his own satisfaction. Although he rejected the idea of an arranged marriage for example, he was not willing to upset his parents by completely ignoring their wishes. He said:

There is the stuff like arranged marriages and so on. I disagree with that, but that doesn't mean that I am totally 100 per cent against it – I am against it 90 per cent but because of my parents you know, I don't want to upset them. No matter what, you know – like, say you found a girl and fell in love, well I'd ask my parents about it first if I did want to get married.

This last sentiment was echoed by other Indian and Pakistani boys. Within the South Asian communities some variation appeared concerning conformity to cultural norms. Part of one conversation with a Pakistani boy went as follows:

Well there's only one problem, I can take a lass home as long as she is my friend, I'm not going out with her or anything like that. But if they [his parents] don't like her they won't let me bring her down home again.

INTERVIEWER: Do you think attitudes are changing, softening, within the community?

It just depends on what type of families you look at. 'Cos my Dad gives me more freedom, you know he doesn't care if neighbours say something or talk about something. He sort of argues against them and he sticks up for me, whether I am wrong or right. But the next door neighbours, if there is anything their family does wrong and somebody tells them about it they get really angry. Like my friends, when they see all these ladies and women and all this English sort coming down to our house, they start getting funny ideas what we are doing.

We have already said that Asian girls have similar difficulties. Most girls in this position had come to terms with conforming to the norms of one culture whilst having contact with another 'I am all right really me, it's not all that difficult for me, 'cos it's our religion and you have to put up with it, don't you?' was one comment. 'In our culture there is less freedom, because they [parents] were given less freedom they are doing the same to us', was another. A third girl said: 'I'd do exactly what my parents have done to me because I think it's very important to keep one's culture. To be identified because when you live in a society it's very important to belong to a society, if you don't belong to something then when you are cast out and get lonely and it's very bad for you'. However, not all the South Asian girls were as willing to conform as these three Pakistani girls.

The Headmaster of one school who particularly understood the problems faced by immigrant girls had noticed that some Asian girls from his school were being 'picked up' by Asian 'taxi drivers' during dinner-time and suspected something 'not quite right' was happening. In response to this observation the researchers pursued this matter when interviewing youngsters. The following extract is typical of a number of transcripts obtained by one (female) interviewer:

PAKISTANI GIRL: Well yes, really but, you know, I don't think they have much to do really about what's going on. Take the Headmaster, he's doing his best really, you know, at playtimes and everything, not to let the girls out you know.

I: But it seems bad if that does happen, surely the girls should have enough sense?

PG: Yes it is happening mostly at dinner times 'cos when I was at school, mostly at dinner times, you know, lads from outside, that were married came outside, outside the school, you know, with their cars. Hanging about for girls and take them to the park and everything.

I: That's quite serious isn't it – especially when it's people who have nothing to do with the school?

PG: That's why most of our Asian girls, you know, when they are at a certain age they leave school. They don't go into the sixth form. It's mainly because of their parents, you know. Well at school nobody will know that so and so has gone to India or Pakistan for this reason, but if you know their parents you know, you know.

Information provided by other youngsters suggests that to some extent the behaviour of these girls is related to their contact with Western moral values. Unfortunately, it appears that in looking for the sexual freedom they perceived among their English peers these girls had alienated themselves from the Asian community.

There was one instance of a white girl suffering 'culture shock', not because of her race but because of her sex. This girl had spent all of her pre-sixth-form education in a single-sex school:

> I couldn't get on with boys at first. I found I just couldn't get on with them being in the lessons. I have only got boys in the geography lessons really, one boy in French lessons and none in English. I found it a bit difficult at first, very self conscious I was and I didn't know how to talk to the boys. I thought they were different, but they are not really.

Apart from offering help and support such as grumbling together, the peer group can be a source of problems and a 'bad influence'.

> One girl in the fifth form, she picked on me and she kept on picking on me every day. I just kept on ignoring her and then she pushed me down the steps. I told the Headteacher, and he took her and told her off. She said if you tell the Headteacher again I'll kick you in again. And she kept on doing that to me again. So I told my parents and they went up to school and told the Headmaster.   (Indian girl)

> To get on you've got to have ambition first, and the will to work. All my mates are on the dole and they love it 'cos they love staying in their beds and going to night clubs and stuff like that. They say there is no jobs going – that is their excuse in life – but I know there is 'cos when I left school there was jobs going. If you were in the right place at the right time, you could get a job.   (West Indian boy)

Unfortunately, as we mentioned before, not every youngster knew how to be 'in the right place at the right time'.

It is not possible, then, to give an overall picture of the relative influence of each of the three elements of the immediate environment – the school, the family, and the peer group – from the interview data. One might say that almost every individual had been influenced, for better or worse, to some extent by each source. No two people or their experiences were identical, however, and, hence, what was an influence for one youngster was not necessarily so for another. The interviews, then, show a complex situation.

Choice at 16+

On reaching the statutory school leaving age, each child was faced with a choice of options. As a West Indian girl said, 'There are four choices: go on a YOPS scheme; get a job; stay 'till sixth form; go to college. And you looked through it and thought, that's not much of a choice.' This girl had found making a decision very difficult, partly because of a lack of good advice at school. Examination of the interviews revealed both ethnic-group and sex differences in the reasons for the youngsters' choices.

Two options – entering the sixth form and going to a College of Further Education – involved further study for examinations. The belief that better qualifications would lead to more job opportunities was widespread amongst the youngsters. For some, qualifications gave access to higher education: 'After my 'A' levels I want to go and get a degree because I don't think there is any point in doing the 'A' levels unless you want to go on a degree course – you might as well just take 'O' levels.' said one English girl. For others, studying further was to enhance qualifications and improve their chances of obtaining work. A youngster with Polish parents said: 'Had I left school I would have been much worse because it is once you leave school you are stuck with that job and if you have got more qualifications, the more money you will be getting afterwards.' A West Indian pupil expressed almost the same sentiments: 'I thought, well, it was harder to get the good jobs and if I went to college I would be one of the really good ones, I'd have a chance to get right to the top'. The idea that examination passes lead to a wider range of job opportunities was summarised by a Pakistani boy who had decided to stay on into the sixth form:

You have got more of a chance and more of a choice the more qualifications you get, so instead of getting stuck to one thing or whatever, if you can grab hold of more qualifications you have got more of a choice.

A substantial proportion (about 40 per cent) of the sixth-formers interviewed had decided to leave school and look for work, but on failing to find full-time employment had returned to school either to improve qualifications or simply to avoid unemployment. This was outlined by a West Indian girl:

> I think a lot of people chose the sixth form because of the job situation, because they didn't want to go through the dole and things. I think it is depressing seeing your friends on the dole anyway – you don't want that to happen to you. Stay on even if its just for the year. You do it 'cos you think you might as well because you are not given anything else.

This statement also shows the 'external' way of reasoning which was more pronounced amongst West Indian and white youngsters. ('External' reasoning is derived from the individual's belief that others have control of his or her life: 'internal' reasoning is when the individual believed he or she has control over life events.) Clearly this girl believes that others both provide the opportunities and restrict the choices. One Indian boy had a clear idea why he should stay on into the sixth form. For him it was not chiefly the qualifications he might get, but the views of prospective employers which may be influenced by his continuance in full-time education.

> Basically what I am trying to do now is staying on in the sixth form so that people think the lad's not losing interest and so that when I go for a job I can say look I am in the sixth form. I am in a situation whereby I am willing to leave if I am offered a good job, but I am not going to be too choosy. So I stayed on in the sixth form so as not to be regarded as a 16 year old who had left school with virtually no education 'cos people who leave school with 5 'O' levels get a job, it is very seldom that they don't and that is why I stayed on in the sixth form and also I took 'A' level economic history and geography and general studies.

Those in the sixth form fall into three categories: those wishing to go to higher education, those wishing to improve qualifications for better jobs and those who wished to leave school but did not because they could find no work. There were ethnic and sex differences in the proportions who stayed at school for these reasons. The majority of white girls interviewed had decided to go to University or other forms of higher education where 'A' levels were necessary, and so in their own minds they had no option but to stay on at school; an exception was the girl who felt that she 'was not old enough for a job'. A similar picture emerged for the white boys where, again, a majority had decided to stay on at school to gain 'A' levels and so entry to higher education. Only one white boy stayed on to avoid unemployment, largely because of 'the thought of the dole queues and terrible career prospects which suddenly hit me towards the latter part of the fifth year'. The other main reason of the white boys was the retaking of 'O' levels after they had got poor grades.

The major reason given by Asian girls for staying on at school was that they had been unsuccessful in getting any type of work and had returned to improve their qualifications and thereby their chances of finding some. To some extent the situation faced by Muslim girls was very different from that of any other group. There was some evidence that parents decided about staying on at school, but their advice to the girls varied. Some parents definitely did not want their children to stay on:

I could have stayed on but you see the way things are with Asian people at school, with girls, they have been very baddies at school reality. You know my parents, some people have told my parents about girls how they have been at school – so my parents have got the idea you see of girls, how they are at school and how they are at home you see. So my parents that's why they didn't tell me to stay on a bit further with my course you see. That's why really. It's one of the main reasons. (Pakistani girl)

Others advised differently:

Yes, they have 'cos they think that you know there's no jobs nowadays for us so they said that you might as well stay on at school and get a higher grade or you know, or get a higher qualification for a better job. (Pakistani girl)

It is interesting that the girl who had been told to leave school by her parents was due to be married by arrangement shortly after the interview.

The reasons given by the South Asian boys tended to centre on the idea that more academic qualifications mean a better career with good prospects. Quite frequently they had no particular purpose but were working to gain better qualifications and hoping that it would help. One Indian boy said:

I am getting a bit restless I think I would like to leave, well I want to leave to get some money and get some experience of working then I think, well I'll get some qualifications first they might just help me, you know.

Despite the general trend, there were one or two Asian pupils who, although they had worked hard at school, were becoming dispirited because they saw others get work before them irrespective of qualifications. This Pakistani boy was beginning to doubt the relationship between qualifications and employment:

I want a job where my academic effort is valid . . . . I don't want to be regarded as a shopkeeper, I could do that anytime. If I had known that, I could have messed about at school. I know people who messed about in the fifth form, no effort whatsoever, and they are in jobs – they are in good jobs which makes me feel degraded when I stand next to them and yet they have not got any 'O' levels.

Generally, the West Indian girls gave the same reasons as the English and South Asian girls combined – they either needed more qualifications to go to college or they disliked the idea of being unemployed. The West Indian boys gave various reasons for staying on at school. Some intended to go on to higher education and were studying for 'A' levels, whilst hoping to improve existing qualifications by, say, retaking 'O' levels. Interestingly, only one West Indian boy had tried to find work and had returned to school after he had been unsuccessful. Another West Indian boy found the decision about staying on in the sixth form very difficult. He seemed a little confused about the value of sixth form education for getting work. He could see that employers may look for criteria other than educational qualifications:

A year is quite enough in the sixth form. I don't think I would stop in two years because when you are 18 – they would want experience and in some jobs it's not brains you want, they wouldn't want you at all, experience – it's experience what counts, in some jobs. And besides they would want you at 16 if they want brains or such. That's what I think anyway.

It can be said, then, that a significant proportion of those who had decided to stay on at school did so because they could not find work and did not want to 'be on the dole'. The proportion of such youngsters was greater for South Asians and West Indians, and this is probably for two reasons: firstly South Asian teenagers tended to have a stronger belief that qualifications would lead to work and secondly, and, perhaps more importantly, many of the black or brown young people had found it harder to get work because of racial prejudice. Experience of such discrimination is discussed later.

This discrimination was a major reason why ethnic minority youngsters stayed on at school, and one West Indian boy said:

> Most of my friends who have got jobs are English – well, white – they have got the jobs probably because they are white. 'Cos all my mates who are Asian or Black as it were, they have gone back to sixth form.

This suggests that some pupils stay on at school, not for academic reasons but because their ethnic characteristics deny other possibilities.

Apart from staying on at school, there were a number of other options, and one of these was going to a college of further education. Views about attending college were mixed and did not seem to characterise any ethnic group. There were those who, like this West Indian girl, dismissed the possibility, though for unusual reasons:

> I don't want to go to college because I go to college on a Monday and I don't like what I see at college. Quite simply it is all people smoking in classrooms and I just don't like that, that is no way to get on. I really think it's too lax, but then school is too strict.

Others had entered college to continue their education instead of in the sixth form where the discipline was more formal.

A third option for those unable to find work was the Youth Opportunities Programme. Generally, these were not highly regarded by the youngsters as the comment of one white boy made only too clear. He said. 'I couldn't get a job and if I went on the dole or Social Security I'd have learnt nothing, except on Youth Opportunities and I didn't want that.' A small number of school-leavers had become resigned to no work on leaving school. When asked what he wanted to do on leaving school a white boy commented 'just take my dole money and see where I go from there.' Such comments were infrequent from those still at school however, and the vast majority had quite high hopes about future possibilities.

The fourth option was to leave school and seek work, and reasons for this varied considerably. Some had very little idea of how difficult finding work can be: one West Indian boy wanted to be a car mechanic, and said:

> If I can't get through as a car mechanic I would not mind working on computers. I don't think it will be too easy getting a job in mechanics, but computers I'll be all right in, I don't think it will be too hard.

Others fully understood the problems of finding work, but saw them more as a challenge. A Ukrainian boy thought so, saying:

> I just wanted to get out and get a job because there weren't many about so I thought well get out there and try and get one.

He reflected the view of most who left school that there was no particular reason for leaving except that it was an option. A considerable proportion (some 70 per cent) could not give one reason why they left school. This suggests that it was just 'accepted' by many without much thought. This trend was more pronounced among the white young people, but it also existed within the other groups.

The final option was only open to girls and applied specifically to Asian girls. This was to leave school and not seek work, but to prepare for marriage. One Pakistani girl aptly summarised the feelings of a small, but significant number of Asian girls:

> I don't think it's important for a girl to get a job. 'Cos anyway when she gets married she'll have kids and that and she only going to look after the home, she won't be going to work. Girls don't have to work you see, men do, it's just like that you see.

Nevertheless, there was some evidence that attitudes towards female employment may be softening, as the following statement indicates:

> I think some do but with religion and being in a Western society it is a bit difficult because in Asia it's women's role to go get married, have children, that's your career and look after them but whereas there it's changing slowly, you notice that 'cos some of my older friends are married, they have got kids, whereas in the sort of younger generation they have got careers and some of them are married and

still haven't had children you know, it's really surprising. Some girls I know they left school at 16, had a child at 17 you know, really surprised at all that but now it's not like that.

Looking for work is a major part of a school-leaver's life. Means of finding it fall roughly into two categories – the 'formal' and the 'informal'. The 'formal' type of employment search concerns a person responding to a vacancy advertised by an employer (including the use of careers' office and job centre in addition to media advertisements). The 'informal' type of job search concerns searching for a vacancy either by approaching employers directly or by exploiting networks of family and friends. A major trend within the qualitative data was that a much larger proportion of those in work had found those jobs informally. One consequence of using informal networks is that they tend to put at a disadvantage those without extensive contacts in established industry. Generally speaking, ethnic minority youngsters do not have access to extensive informal networks as do the indigenous community. It should be noted, however, that in certain circumstances the dependence of employers on informal ways of recruiting employees is illegal. A number of ethnic minority school-leavers commented on their inability to exploit such networks. For example an Indian boy said 'there is the contacts element, you don't need the academic experience for the job – it is just you have got to have the contacts there – word of mouth – I have not got anything like that.' Another boy had decided to approach employers directly after having no success replying to advertisements. He suspected, however, that some employers practised racial discrimination in employee selection. Because of this he tried to hide his race:

> Well I rang up once to a firm and I spoke very politely you know, and they got me an interview. They got a shock though 'cos I said my name was David Jones or something like that. And he [the employer] sort of stared at me you know, he went and asked if the secretary had heard my name properly. He made excuses and said he would ring me later if he could give me the job – but I didn't hear.   (Indian boy with the surname 'Singh').

It would be wrong to criticise this employer for not offering the boy a job – for he had been given false information – but it does confirm that racially prejudiced employers exist in West Yorkshire.

This Indian boy was not the only interviewee who believed that his race was the cause of his problems in finding work. Another Indian boy changed his opinions through personal experience:

> I remember seeing some of the applicants, and prior to that my Mum and Dad used to say that racial prejudice exists and I used not to believe them because of my friends and the teachers. As soon as I started to experience this situation where I was short-listed and did not get the job. I started feeling sort of rejected and bitter.

Such experiences and attitudes were not limited to South Asian boys. One Pakistani girl commented:

> You see they offered this work at _____ You know at school well there were five of us who applied for it. Three Asian girls applied for it, including me, and two English girls. And _____ accepted the two English ones and said no to us and I don't think that's fair.

Not all the ethnic minority youngsters had experienced racial prejudice first hand. Indeed, one second generation West Indian boy, whose own personal aspiration was to be the first Black player for Yorkshire County Cricket Club, did not believe that racial prejudice was a problem in getting work and attempted to 'explain away' the idea:

> It depends how you look at it – If you go for a job thinking that the man's racialist, you probably won't get it. And then if you don't get it, it breeds more doesn't it?.

This comment was exceptional and was a reflection of this particular boy who had left school after finding a job through his own personal 'connections'.

No matter what the cause of unemployment, the effects on the individual were similar. After some time without a job (and the actual time varied quite considerably between individuals) the youngster became dispirited or de-motivated. This was expressed in many ways:

> Now I have been rejected from so many jobs all I want to do now is get a job. I am asking people what is the fault with me. Why can't I get a job.   (Indian boy)

I went down the the Careers Office and the Job Centre, but there was nothing there. I'd try for any job, so that's what I've been doing. I've had replies – I went for an interview last Wednesday, but I didn't get it.   (White boy)

Yes – I feel really funny now, like going down to the job centre. I don't even like to meet my friends sometimes because they all know what they are doing don't they. Look at me, I'm here, I've done nothing really. Before in school I used to be the one who knew everything, but now I feel as though I don't know anything. I don't like to meet them a lot.   (Pakistani girl).

I am slowly giving up. May, June, July, August and September – it's five months now and I have had one interview – it's demoralising and I hate sitting at home all day.   (White girl)

I've been round to a couple of places enquiring but they had no vacancies. I'm bored, it's really boring. I watch telly and stay in bed all day.   (White girl)

The interview data, therefore, strongly supports the findings of the self-esteem inventory: unemployment does precipitate low self-esteem. Some unemployed youngsters tended to attribute their unemployment to factors beyond their control – the most common being a general lack of work.

One trend which was evident from the interview data was that South Asian youngsters who had not achieved highly expressed more regret than others about their school's work. Moreover, these youngsters tended not to blame the school for their difficulty in finding work. 'Well it was a good school really – it has got a lot of opportunity but I think I could have done a little bit better. I just look back now and think "Oh! how could I have missed those opportunities there." I try not to think about it now', said one Pakistani boy who had been unemployed for some time. South Asian youngsters tended to take responsibility for failure (particularly in examinations) and this is shown by this comment from an Indian girl:

In the third and fourth [forms] I didn't really pay attention in school, I was one of them stupid types, I didn't like school much. But in the 5th form when I realised that we need these qualifications I tried my best and I came out with good marks, good but still they weren't good enough. I was disappointed.

Although a substantial proportion of youngsters interviewed held the belief that better examination results lead to better job opportunities, some who had left school and found work did not think that academic qualifications were the only criteria used by employers during employee selection.

> I have been reading all the papers you see. You need experience, you have got the qualifications, then you need five years' experience behind you. Experience is vital really apart from qualifications as well.   (Pakistani boy)

Some youngsters had found themselves in the vicious circle of needing experience to get a job, and needing a job to gain experience.

> Well, first is that I don't have any experience. Secondly is that they wanted someone who knows about that thing, and sometimes it's a matter of age. Sometimes they make you take a test, you might pass or fail. You don't know, but they say that you haven't succeeded.
>   (Pakistani boy)

A further consideration about finding work concerns restrictions placed on some Asian girls by parents insisting on conformity to cultural or religious norms. In some cases this started at school where the advice of a careers teacher or officer conflicted with the values of the home:

> I had two interviews with the careers teacher and they asked me what to do. I said helping old people and nursery nursing and so on. Then they told me to go on work experience. My parents don't allow that, they say work experience is mixed for girls and boys and my parents say that it's no good thing being with boys because boys are . . ., boys are different than girls.   (Pakistani girl)

Although fairly infrequent, such sentiments were of major importance to some Muslim girls, particularly when this prevented them from having certain types of work which otherwise they would have enjoyed:

> I could have been a nurse – there are girls who take City and Guilds who go to different hospitals in Bradford. But if I took on nursing I would have to wear a skirt which is against my religion. I'd have liked that very much.   (Pakistani girl)

There was one [a job vacancy] up at where my father works – they are all men there, so he wouldn't let me work there. (Pakistani girl)

In general, there was little regret expressed to the interviewers by South Asian girls, who unquestioningly tended to accept the restrictions placed upon them.

Commentary on the Interview Experience

Towards the end of an interview, the youngster was often asked what he or she thought of being interviewed, and whether it had been worrying. This allowed one West Indian boy to express a more general picture of how he would like to be treated:

It depends if you rub someone up the wrong way, it's the tone of your voice. If someone starts shouting at you, you are not going to like it. If I'd come in here and you had started shouting at me I'm not going to start talking on there as if we are good friends. It's just how you get treated like an equal then everything is all right but if you get treated like a nutter then things make it more. If you get more attention than others it makes it worse. It just makes it worse to me. You just want the same as everyone – same as everyone wants the same for himself.

Finally, one white girl was promised a quotation in the final report of the research for the following comment (she had not been told the purpose or the source of the research).

I don't mind – I'd say I'd enjoyed it as long as the results are published – so much of things like government things are being hidden and don't tell the whole story so I am all for them if they are going to find out something and if the results are published and people are going to take notice of them and if something is wrong try and put it right.

A summary of the findings of Chapters 7 and 8 is given in Appendix 5.

9 Reflections and Implications

In reviewing the empirical research reported in earlier chapters, we should stress that this book is not intended to be a research monograph, but rather a discussion and commentary, a contribution to the continuing debate about ethnicity and educational achievement in British schools. We hope that the findings obtained will fill some of the gaps in the Swann Report (HMSO, 1985).

We have shown that the antecedents of educational achievement are different between ethnic groups. While such a finding should alert teachers to the dangers of a naively monocultural approach, it would be equally dangerous to recommend any particular approach on the basis of these findings. First of all, it could be that our findings cannot be generalised beyond the West Yorkshire region; it may also be that the findings are unreliable in some cases because of the relatively small samples involved.

What is certain, however, is that the position of ethnic relations in West Yorkshire or elsewhere in Britain, is a dynamic one involving both structural and personal changes. At a structural level the advent of high rates of youth unemployment has changed the perceptions which young people have of themselves as achievers and job-finders, and has also altered their educational and occupational strategies.

At a personal, family and community level there is some evidence that the second and third generation descendants of the original migrants are becoming more sophisticated in their educational and occupational orientations, learning from (but not emulating) their white peers.

Given this reality it is important that teachers and others consulting the findings of this empirical work, should not naively commit the 'fallacy of composition'. This involves the generalisation from the characteristics of a few members of a group to the whole of that class. But statistical results of the kind presented here involve many 'false positions' – members of the group whose antecedents of achievement are quite different from those of their fellow ethnic group members. It is more important, in fact, that teachers should operate without stereotyped and prejudiced conceptions of what the motivation and aspirations of a particular ethnic group are. The most important task for teachers is to teach *all* pupils well and effectively, and without stereotype or prejudice.

The research we have reported has a number of acknowledged weaknesses. We have offered a complex model of antecedents of achievement, but we have not adequately tested such a model with our data. Moreover, although the model requires input from the disciplines of educational psychology, sociology and anthropology, we have framed our research firmly within the traditions of academic social psychology. The contextual variables and value orientations we have identified owe little to the ethnographic approach. Similarly, our method of using personal interviews to enrich the statistical base of the research will do little to satisfy those who are grounded in ethno-methodological techniques.

A perceived weakness is the use of achievement in examinations as a dependent variable. Being allowed to enter for examinations may be, as Taylor (1976) argued, a reflection of how schools perceive certain pupils, rather than a pure measure of achievement as such. One way of investigating this would be to carry out a between-schools analysis of a number of schools admitting similar proportions of pupils from different ethnic groups and from similar backgrounds. But in order to undertake that kind of research we would have needed a much larger pool of co-operative schools than we originally had.

In retrospect we regret not having divided 'white' pupils into constituent minority ethnic groups – traditional Yorkshire English; Scots, Welsh or Irish descent; and descent from Northern, Southern and Eastern European backgrounds. Another growing 'ethnic group' consists of children of mixed backgrounds, a reflection of the growing number of ethnically mixed marriages. Some 20 per cent of marriages involving a black person occur in a black–white marriage – a far higher rate than in the United States (Bagley, 1979) – and the percentage probably has increased since 1979. Moreover, such marriages produce children, neither black nor white, with a clear identity and sense of purpose in life (Bagley and Young, 1984). The debate on multicultural education in Britain has not taken proper account of this phenomenon, and groupings of pupils into 'black' and 'white' or 'West Indian' and 'British' for purposes of comparison are becoming increasingly meaningless. The dilemma of a strategy which reflects this, however, is that numbers for analysis in any one group become rather small. Nevertheless we are convinced that in any future research the term 'ethnic minority' should not become a euphemism for groups originating from the New Commonwealth.

While the acknowledgement of the multiplicity of ethnic groups in Britain – both white and black – has implications for emerging models of cultural pluralism, a paradox in this assumption should be recognised. We have implicitly assumed that, notwithstanding the search for specific factors with ethnic groups, the standard of achievement is *monocultural*. Of course, in a completely plural society each ethnic group would have institutionally separate arrangements and would establish its own schools and examination boards. Whether such a development is possible or even desirable is a difficult question to answer. There are some Muslims who question whether the interests of their community would be better served by separate schools. Perhaps a comment here from a Muslim girl is pertinent:

> I am a practising Muslim girl of 17 years and I go to Belle Vue Girls' School in Bradford . . . I strongly oppose the proposition . . . concerning the establishment of Muslim schools. Many of my fellow Muslim pupils and I believe that this is wrong . . . There are many practising Muslim girls and their families with whom I have discussed this matter who have said they oppose the idea of totally Muslim schools.
>
> (A Muslim Sixth Form girl's letter to *The Times Educational Supplement*, 10 June 1983).

We tend to favour the approach of Swann (HMSO, 1985) which advocates a balance, breadth and equity within a broadly 'pluralist' approach; this would both educate the dominant majority in the etiquette and folkways of multiculturalism, and make schools acceptable arenas of personal development and educational achievement for *all* ethnic groups. As Swann argues (p. 519) the danger of failing to address adequately the question of 'education for all' would be a stimulus for certain ethnic groups to set up separate schools. But such moves might well accentuate the ethnocentrism of the remaining all-white schools.

Some readers may question our use of a general measure of self-esteem as a possible antecedent of achievement within each cultural group. Measures of self-esteem, like measures of achievement, may not be culture-free. But to support the measure used we would point out that we have demonstrated the reliability of the measures of self-esteem used in various ethnic groups, including Indian adolescents in India (Verma and Bagley, 1982). We used a measure of general self-esteem, rather than measures of self-concept of ability because in our previous empirical work it was this measure rather than special sub-scales which predicted achievement most consistently (Bagley, Verma, Mallick and Young, 1979). Nevertheless, we have not used identity theory and related measures because the current situation in British society is fluid with the dynamic of change. While self-esteem will be likely to remain an important antecedent of achievement, the manner in which it is incorporated into identity in various ethnic groups will almost certainly not remain the same.

A puzzling variable which has hardly been addressed in this research is that of sex. For example, why is it that when sexes are compared, social class predicts achievement in males but not in females? This result seems to relate across more than one ethnic group. Is it possible that sex is a more important basis for social differentiation and of particular types of achievement-related factors than ethnicity? This is an important question for future research.

We should also acknowledge that this research has not explored with any adequacy the variable of religion, which might also cut across the variable of ethnicity. For example, being Catholic, Jewish, Protestant, Muslim, Hindu or Sikh may be an important antecedent of achievement, rather than the broader and rather over-inclusive concept of ethnicity.

One particular cause for concern that emerged during the research was the suggestion that large numbers of South Asian children tended to visit Pakistan and Bangladesh for periods ranging from weeks to years. Whilst it can be seen that continuity of education in British schools is disrupted (with possible consequences later) such experience can be immensely valuable if utilised by schools constructively and positively. At the moment, however, there seems to be no solution to this issue which can be universally accepted.

Finally, in future research, as well as operationalising the variables of sex and religion more fully, we should also like to include traditional variables such as family size, housing conditions and amount and type of parental education as antecedents of achievement.

REFLECTIONS

Recently much public attention has been drawn to the question of underachievement among ethnic minority children. Much of this has arisen following the publication of the Rampton Report (HMSO, 1981), the Interim Report of the Committee of Enquiry into the Education of Children of Ethnic Minority Groups, and of the Swann Report (HMSO, 1985), the final report of this Committee.

The Rampton Report had as its prime focus the circumstances and experiences of West Indian children in Britain and therefore tended to play down those of children from other ethnic minority groups, notably those from various parts of South Asia, China etc. In view of the headlines that the Brixton, Toxteth and Bristol disturbances attracted, the emphasis in the Rampton Report was, in one sense, not surprising.

One effect, however, was that the report did nothing to discourage the trend to apply the term 'black' to all the non-white population of Britain. While there may be a certain justification for grouping together non-whites (in that many non-whites may experience similar social and environmental disadvantages, such as discrimination prejudice, urban deprivation and poor housing) the 'black' stereotype tends to engender the belief that all non-whites are completely similar. Such a stereotype overlooks the wide range of socio-cultural traditions and values held by different non-whites. These traditions and values are an important element of the life-styles of those people and affect their attitude to broader society.

The Rampton Report also attracted criticism because its findings rested heavily on anecdotal and experiential evidence rather than on evidence built up from systematic social research.

The research reported in the present volume has tried to present a series of findings that consider the variety of ethnic and cultural backgrounds from which Britain's adolescents come and through a carefully constructed research model to analyse how those factors mediate the process of educational achievement.

This research derives from three related studies, the focus being on adolescents in the Leeds/Bradford area of West Yorkshire. All youngsters were either in their last year of compulsory schooling or had just gone beyond that stage. In all the studies the research design employed an admixture of quantitative (questionnaire and test) and qualitative (interview) techniques; these were used to give the studies breadth and depth. The total sample covered by the studies exceeded

1500 youngsters who were or had been pupils at nine different schools drawn from two adjacent Local Authorities.

The belief from the start was that the responses to the last year of compulsory schooling (and the various options beyond that stage) were likely to be mediated by the differing cultural backgrounds of the young people being studied and accordingly, they were not categorised as white and non-white but by the ethnic group (e.g., white, Indian). Such a design facilitated the examination of educational achievement of ethnic minority adolescents, since the data collected offered information on many factors relating to achievement.

The research findings were built on a model that sought to analyse the impact of a wide range of factors – from school, home, peer group and cultural background – in a new way. The model had a number of underlying assumptions which it was thought would offer a more comprehensive picture of the patterns of achievement than hitherto obtained by other studies in the field. Two assumptions were considered paramount. The first was that educational achievement – whether expressed in terms of public examination success, type of employment obtained or even in terms of personal satisfaction – was the product of a complex interaction of educational, cultural, familial and psychological factors; and this interaction process – the impact of these factors on an individual – was likely to be unique. Obvious limitations existed in following such a theoretical model to its logical conclusions. Given the uniqueness of the individual interaction process, however, it was essential to strike a balance between the broad and the narrow focus so that the model could have useful application.

This application was governed by the second major underlying assumption. This was that the individual interaction processes were likely to have more in common with the cultural background from which the individual came than by the crude categorisation of white and non-white. A practical model has to offer findings capable of generalisation and enough flexibility to consider the possible impact of distinctive cultural variations on individual achievement. To create such a model it was decided to subject the data to analyses *within*, rather than *between* ethnic groups.

When examining the education of ethnic minority children previous studies have tended to relate the performance of the group or groups to that of all children in the area or to the relative performance of one group with another or others. Such inter-ethnic analysis fails to allow for possibly significant factors affecting performance among children from a particular ethnic group. Consequently, it tends to obscure or ignore factors mediating on the individual interaction process. More importantly in broad terms, *intra*-ethnic analysis, by highlighting factors most typical of high and low achievement from members of that ethnic group, would indicate the differing importance of factors relating to achievement for different ethnic groups.

As opposed to simply the level of achievement, the processes of educational achievement are dependent upon culture. Examination by intra-ethnic analysis of the interplay of social, educational, cultural, familial and psychological factors mediating on achievement showed distinct variations between high and low achievers of one ethnic group when compared with those of the other groups. The findings, therefore, were consistent with our contention that the term 'non-white' or 'ethnic minority' adolescent was simplistic when examining the educational performance of youngsters from different ethnic groups. This also reinforces one of our assumptions underlying the research, namely, that of the uniqueness of particular cultural experiences.

The varying importance of those factors on understanding the achievement of youngsters is borne out in our findings which are reported in Chapters Seven and Eight. These showed, for example, that in terms of perceived parental interest in their child's schooling, *maternal* interest was a significant discriminator between high and low achievement for white and West Indian youngsters, whereas for Bangladeshi and Indian youngsters perceived *paternal* interest was significant. In further contrast, among Pakistani youngsters, *both* paternal and maternal interest were significant. Similarly, perceived sources of help in passing examinations were not always significant in all groups; sources reaching significance varied from group to group. Even the school attendance/absence factor – a discriminator in all groups – was not of equal importance to every group. Indeed the factor of school attendance/absence has different manifestations: illness, care of younger siblings, extended visits to the country of origin, truancy because of disillusionment with school or because of school problems. Ethnic groups (including our broad group of 'whites') differ in characteristics and experience so that even the groupings obscure a variety of important cultural variations.

Other patterns emerging from the analysis of data had more general implications. These relate to the commitments to education and the 16+ options. They have a wider bearing on educational and occupational policy as well as on individual achievement.

Equating examination success with the prospect of obtaining employment held true for more than two-thirds of the total sample, although the proportion of West Indian teenagers holding this view was considerably lower. Motivation levels were found to be greater among South Asian groups than in the white and West Indian groups. Evidence suggests that motivation levels among the South Asian groups appeared to be derived more from fear of failure than from the desire to succeed. West Indian young people tended to think that having a good school record was a better means of obtaining employment than examination success. Expressed intentions to enter further or higher education, as opposed to seeking work at 16, varied from group to group. For example, two-thirds of the white youngsters preferred to try the employment option, compared with only one-third of South Asian and West Indian young people.

Whatever individual considerations may motivate such intentions, clearly there are important implications here, not only for the classroom where youngsters from different backgrounds sit together, but also for educational provision.

A further factor from the findings that showed distinct inter-ethnic difference was in the approach to obtaining employment. There appeared to be two distinct networks, which we have dubbed the 'formal' and the 'informal'. Although this is not a novel finding, the implications of it in terms of this research were considered important in an ethnic minority context. White youngsters seemed to have far greater access to the informal network than other ethnic groups. Such a network (family connections, direct approaches to employers) appeared to override educational qualifications and placed those who relied on the formal network of school (vacancies advertised in the press and elsewhere, Careers Office and Job Centre) at a disadvantage. While one should not discourage individual initiative, there are grounds for increasing feelings of alienation developing amongst those from the ethnic minorities who rely more heavily on the formal network in a steadily shrinking employment market. Such a finding has · considerable implications for the careers education programme in schools if ethnic minority youngsters are to try to exploit the informal network as well as the formal one.

After discussion of some of the data-based findings from our research, it is appropriate to locate them within a broader context. The observations that follow come not so much from analysis of data, but rather from having worked on the research project for six years and living where the research was located.

In broad terms there appear to be signs for optimism about the situation of people from the ethnic minority communities. It would be wrong to disguise the fact that many ethnic minority people still face many disadvantages such as poor housing, and racial discrimination in employment. However, over the six years there appear to have been an increasing local awareness of what people from ethnic minorities are adding to the quality of life. This awareness, however flimsy at present, seems to come from more personal and direct experience by the majority group with individuals from the ethnic minorities rather than the indirect and often anecdotal knowledge about ethnic minority communities which previously existed. If the level of awareness – the product of inter-ethnic contact – continues, there are important implications for employment and education quite apart from any other social considerations. Our discussions with local employers, the careers service and teachers all point to an increasing awareness of what individuals from the ethnic minority can contribute to larger society. Applicants for jobs in firms having experience of ethnic minority employees are now being judged more on that experience than on pre-conceived stereotypes. Personnel officers we talked to also mentioned ethnic minority employees adjusting to the employment patterns and promotional structures within their firms. If this process continues, then there should be increasing hopes for greater social mobility. In turn this should increase the validity of educational achievement and subsequent employment for ethnic minority youngsters.

The process of adaptation to living in Britain for the children's parents – many of whom migrated to the area – is not without its problems. This appears to have been particularly so where parental interpretation of the home culture has been inflexible, especially concerning the upbringing of girls. Much inter-generational conflict has been reported because of the clash between the wider English culture to which the young people are exposed at school and at play and that of their parents. Such cases obviously attract more attention than those where the whole family has accommodated itself to this mixed cultural situation. In these situations younger siblings have advantages over their elder ones.

One dark cloud threatens the whole view. This is the present economic situation with all its implications not only for employment, but also for education and other social services. If the situation deteriorates further, there is the risk that much of the increasing inter-cultural awareness that we have observed will be swept aside by

narrow self-interest. Remarkably, however, there is some evidence that as youth unemployment effects all ethnic groups, there is developing a shared commitment amongst youth about external forces which deny young people adequate reward for striving in school. Thus the 1981 'riots' were not black versus white riots, but disturbances involving ethnically mixed groupings of youth who were in conflict with established authorities.

IMPLICATIONS

The impact of cultural and immediate family background on the ethnic minority child's values and attitudes to education in general and to school in particular, probably are more marked than those of the white child. Moreover, the impact of those factors on ethnic minority children is likely to show distinct variation between ethnic groups. The categorisation of minority youngsters into ethnic groups showed a number of such variations from group to group: each group seems likely to contain other significant variations because of differing cultural traditions and cultural adaptation to life in Britain. The need for appreciating and understanding those potential variations cannot be over-stressed. There would appear to be a particular need for all those dealing with ethnic minority youngsters to be sensitised to this.

The cultural values of the school, particularly the informal ones, may be dissonant with those of the home. Hence there are potentially greater risks of inter-generational conflict (youngster and parent) which may affect the attitude to school and educational achievement of the ethnic minority adolescent.

If a climate of increasing inter-ethnic tolerance and understanding is allowed to grow, there appears to be more chance of ethnic minority adaptation to a new 'cultural' climate; this will facilitate freer movement for the youngster between the cultural climates of school, peers and home.

If our perception of a growth in inter-cultural awareness among both the ethnic minority groups and those in the white group – in schools and at work – is not false, we would expect to see a reduction in 'racial discrimination' and in perceived racial prejudice. We doubt that these can ever be eliminated entirely, but believe that their effects will be gradually reduced.

Attempts are proceeding to improve the quality and validity of careers education and advice offered in schools and through the careers service. That process should consider the impact of differing cultural and family backgrounds on the performance and self-preservation of ethnic minority youngsters. Thought also should be given to preparing minority youngsters seeking work not only to use formal channels, but to seek out informal ones too.

While no specific findings relating to the school curriculum arose from the research, the issues of multicultural education came to our attention while conducting this investigation. Any programmes that increase intercultural understanding and promote intercultural interaction can, in our view, only help to foster the climate of tolerance referred to earlier.

Some elements of educational provision already considered have implications for policy makers. In addition, there are two other major issues which should be dealt with here: separate schools and alternatives to youth employment.

While the issue of separate schools was not a specific item for study in this research, nonetheless it is an issue which related to our research. Moreover, it is a topic which was raised with us by some people aware of the nature of the research.

Although advocating the creation of separate schools might appear to be consistent with our basic philosophy of a proper respect for particular cultural and religious traditions, such action might well tend to heighten differences between certain ethnic minority youngsters and others. This might have an adverse effect on youngsters of that cultural or religious persuasion, and, if the number of such separate schools was extensive, it would tend to delay intercultural understanding.

It would be hard to deny separate schools on principle, especially in a British context which had both a long and honoured tradition of religious tolerance and of secular schools existing simultaneously with religious ones. It would be difficult, however, for us to support the view sometimes expressed that national or local government should make financial provision to create separate schools. Many existing religious schools have been granted voluntary-aided status. We would not be against the principle of offering voluntary-aided status to secular schools created initially out of a corporate will in a particular community. This should only be so if the Secretary of State for Education were satisfied about the standard of education offered by such schools in relation to national norms.

This study was concerned with the educational achievement of ethnic minority youngsters in the Leeds/Bradford area. A logical

extension to the research would be a series of related studies conducted in other areas of Britain with a multi-ethnic population. Such studies might well show interesting variations on the present findings perhaps because of differing demographic and other related factors.

We have already said that the intra-ethnic model used here has limitations. The development of a more sophisticated model might allow subtler and yet distinctive cultural variations than those allowed by categorisation by ethnic group. Such a model would increase knowledge and awareness of the rich cultural variations that exist in Britain's plural society.

Further insights into the position of ethnic minority youngsters in society could come from comparative studies in Britain and elsewhere. Britain is a member of the European Economic Community in which there is the principle of free movement between member countries for nationals. A comparative study of areas with ethnic minority populations in Britain and, for example, West Germany or France, could have important implications not only for national social policy but also for that of the EEC.

Appendix 1:   Annexe to Chapter 7

TABLES OF RESULTS

TABLE 7.1   *Expected examination entry by ethnic group and sex* (1982–3 Data)

		No Exams at all	GCE[1] 'O' level		CSEs[2]		Others[3]	
			1–4	5–9	1–4	5–9	1 + 2	3–6
			(all shown as percentages)					
All	(N = 394)	14.2	29.4	18.4	42.7	31.2	20.9	19.6
White	(N = 143)	14.3	29.5	18.4	38.1	33.6	15.1	21.6
Pakistani	(N = 73)	16.9	22.1	23.7	57.6	15.3	38.9	6.8
Bangladeshi	(N = 44)	26.7	20.1	13.4	20.1	19.3	20.0	20.0
Indian	(N = 67)	4.7	46.4	9.4	48.9	32.7	32.5	30.5
West Indian	(N = 65)	10.5	30.0	20.0	80.0	10.0	10.0	15.0
Males	(N = 197)	14.4	24.9	15.3	41.2	26.8	39.5	11.3
Females	(N = 197)	14.1	33.2	21.5	42.8	34.5	36.7	22.0

Analysis of variance: $F = 7.517$, $df = 2$, $p = 0.006$
1. General Certificate of Education (Ordinary level)
2. Certificate of Secondary Education
3. Other examinations: (a) Business Education Certificate (BEC)
                               (b) Royal Society of Arts (RSA)
                               (c) Technical Education Certificate (TEC)

TABLE 7.2 *Multiple regression factors relating to achievement: white sample (N = 143)*

Variable	r with achievement	F to enter regression	% of variance
Time away from school	0.362	41.958	14.6
General-self self-esteem	0.119	0.108	<1.0
Social-self-peers self-esteem	0.091	0.097	<1.0
School-academic self-esteem	0·195	5.408	1.8
Home-parents self-esteem	0.074	0.537	<1.0
Father's interest	0.058	0.654	<1.0
Mother's interest	0.104	1.939	<1.0
Enjoyment of school	0.231	2.592	<1.0
Total			18.5

NOTE: 'Achievement' is defined by the number of passes in external examinations.

TABLE 7.3 *Multiple regression of factors relating to achievement: Pakistani sample (N = 73)*

Variable	r with achievement	F to enter regression	% of variance
Time away from school	0.411	9.980	16.9
General-self self-esteem	0.255	0.715	<1.0
Social-self-peers self-esteem	0.279	2.027	2.6
School-academic self-esteem	0·035	1.773	2.4
Home-parents self-esteem	0.216	0.001	<1.0
Father's interest	0.205	0.024	<1.0
Mother's interest	0.365	8.002	11.9
Enjoyment of school	0.262	5.782	7.8
Total			42.5

TABLE 7.4 *Multiple regression of factors relating to achievement: Indian sample (N = 67)*

Variable	r with achievement	F to enter regression	% of variance
Time away from school	0.459	10.411	21.1
General-self self-esteem	0.318	0.793	1.4
Social-self-peers self-esteem	0.228	0.664	1.2
School-academic self-esteem	0·389	4.757	8.8
Home-parents self-esteem	0.023	1.029	1.7
Father's interest	0.064	1.916	3.5
Mother's interest	0.028	0.350	<1.0
Enjoyment of school	0.224	1.075	1.9
Total			40.6

TABLE 7.5   *Multiple regression of factors relating to achievement: Bangladeshi sample ($N = 44$)*

Variable	r with achievement	F to enter regression	% of variance
Time away from school	0.191	6.590	20.2
General-self self-esteem	0.091	0.005	<1.0
Social-self-peers self-esteem	0.065	0.488	1.6
School-academic self-esteem	0·416	3.363	15.1
Home-parents self-esteem	0.202	0.984	3.3
Father's interest	0.268	0.658	2.1
Mother's interest	0.367	0.052	<1.0
Enjoyment of school	0.557	5.837	31.0
Total			73.3

TABLE 7.6   *Multiple regression of factors relating to achievement: West Indian sample ($N = 65$)*

Variable	r with achievement	F to enter regression	% of variance
Time away from school	0.328	0.059	<1.0
General-self self-esteem	0.410	3.643	16.8
Social-self-peers self-esteem	0.228	0.035	<1.0
School-academic self-esteem	0·181	2.028	6.3
Home-parents self-esteem	0.309	0.032	<1.0
Father's interest	0.346	0.012	<1.0
Mother's interest	0.389	8.381	27.5
Enjoyment of school	0.134	1.884	5.5
Total			56.1

TABLE 7.7   *Multiple regression of factors relating to achievement: whole sample ($N = 394$)*

Variable	r with achievement	F to enter regression	% of variance
Time away from school	0.372	60.788	13.8
General-self self-esteem	0.164	0.796	1.0
Social-self-peers self-esteem	0.139	4.473	<1.0
School-academic self-esteem	0·149	0.283	<1.0
Home-parents self-esteem	0.069	0.389	<1.0
Father's interest	0.097	0.608	<1.0
Mother's interest	0.149	8.916	2.0
Enjoyment of school	0.166	1.544	<1.0
Total			17.6

TABLE 7.8 χ^2 Values for median split of achievement compared with predictor variables by sex and ethnic group

Variable	Whole Sample	White	Pakistani	Bangladeshi	Indian	West Indian	Male	Female
General-self self-esteem	6.313*	5.588*	1.702	0.301	1.221	4.892*	13.649**	0.994
Social-self-peers self-esteem	5.930*	4.356*	2.804	0.452	1.683	1.002	0.796	0.112
Home-parents self-esteem	1.565	0.131	1.909	0.092	0.201	2.811	0.373	0.012
School-academic self-esteem	8.008**	8.233**	0.589	0.563	0.292	5.331*	9.028**	0.225
Total self-esteem	9.698***	8.679***	2.527	1.003	1.815	4.222*	8.319**	3.405
Home language	0.929	—	4.635*	3.21	1.688	—	2.735	0.022
Social class	10.940**	7.413*	6.810*	3.200	2.361	1.396	11.322**	0.895
Father's interest in education	10.750*	3.009	7.654*	6.514*	6.201*	1.593	11.256**	1.805
Mother's interest in education	11.254*	5.078*	8.098**	1.607	1.394	6.731*	8.118**	5.549*
Perceived help from teachers	4.301*	4.806*	1.105	0.827	1.922	2.913	3.010	0.655
Perceived help from parents	15.556***	13.806***	0.133	0.341	0.004	0.359	4.576*	4.662*
Perceived help from other pupils	7.201**	3.155	1.387	1.035	0.505	1.932	2.211	4.577*
Perceived help from friends	1.077	3.711*	0.042	0.762	0.009	0.541	0.045	1.474
Perceived help from school	5.138*	3.862*	5.175*	0.403	0.813	1.933	1.280	2.419
Perceived help from siblings	30.995***	27.027***	5.175*	0.159	0.384	0.029	8.744**	18.599**
Perceived help from others	2.406	0.545	—	—	—	—	0.062	0.822
Perceived hindrance from teachers	0.036	0.186	—	0.243	0.340	—	0.900	0.067
Perceived hindrance from parents	0.098	0.002	0.519	0.336	0.340	—	0.001	0.001
Perceived hindrance from other pupils	5.098*	0.311	1.156	1.689	0.065	1.219	0.038*	3.883*
Perceived hindrance from friends	2.255	0.151	0.737	0.156	0.056	0.765	0.202	0.013

continued overleaf

TABLE 7.8 – *continued*

Variable	Whole sample	White	Pakistani	Bangladeshi	Indian	West Indian	Male	Female
Perceived hindrance from school	1.809	0.002	—	0.336	0.010	0.912	0.008	0.002
Perceived hindrance from siblings	0.848	1.981	0.146	0.797	0.086	0.830	0.198	2.852
Perceived hindrance from others	0.065	0.062	—	1.106	0.033	0.651	0.008	0.109
Enjoyment of school	33.312**	25.581**	7.377*	3.194	5.663*	0.286	16.882**	16.826**
Time away from school	43.710**	30.940**	18.217**	8.756*	11.176**	5.333*	19.764**	21.627**

* significant at 5% level
** significant at 1% level

TABLE 7.9   *'t'-test analysis of MAIS scores by ethnic group and sex*

	Mean	Standard deviation	t.	p.
White	293.22	36.18		
South Asian	313.2	29.90	2.54	<0.05
Male	295.51	26.28		
Female	310.51	40.143	2.07	<0.05

TABLE 7.10   *Cross-tabulation of 'enjoyment of school' by ethnic group and sex*
(shown as percentages)

	A great deal	A lot	Some	A little	Not at all
All	19.8	41.0	18.8	10.7	9.8
White	9.1	43.0	22.4	13.1	12.2
Pakistani	39.9	37.3	10.2	10.2	3.4
Bangladeshi	40.0	26.7	26.7	—	6.7
West Indian	35.0	35.0	10.0	—	20.0
Indian	39.5	44.2	9.3	4.7	2.3
Male	13.8	37.8	20.9	13.8	13.8
Female	27.0	44.9	16.2	7.0	4.9

χ^2 across ethnic group = 65.495 ($p<.01$)
χ^2 across sex   = 24.024 ($p<.01$)

TABLE 7.11   *Belief that examination success leads to employment by ethnic group and sex*
(shown as percentages)

	A great deal	A fair amount	Some	A little	Not at all
All	28.6	40.7	13.1	10.4	6.1
White	25.0	45.8	14.0	9.5	5.7
Pakistani	34.5	34.5	8.6	15.5	6.9
Bangladeshi	33.3	53.3	6.7	6.7	0.0
Indian	33.1	23.8	23.8	7.1	7.1
West Indian	25.0	25.5	10.0	25.5	15.0
Male	25.0	40.8	12.3	11.4	8.8
Female	33.0	40.5	14.1	9.2	2.7

χ^2 across ethnic groups = 40.868 ($p = 0.0172$)
χ^2 across sex   = 10.458 ($p = 0.0632$)

TABLE 7.12   *Expected responses to examination failure by ethnic group and sex*
(shown as percentages)

	Retake at school	Retake at college	Not retake
All	48.3	4.5	47.2
White	46.8	4.0	49.2
Pakistani	66.1	5.4	28.6
Bangladeshi	57.1	—	42.9
Indian	63.4	4.9	22.0
West Indian	41.2	17.6	41.2
Male	48.3	2.5	49.3
Female	55.2	6.0	38.8

χ^2 across ethnic groups = 17.853 ($p = 0.042$)
χ^2 across sex   = 6.442 ($p = 0.048$)

TABLE 7.13   *Intentions on leaving school, by ethnic group and sex*
(shown as percentages)

	Get a job	Higher education	Further education	Other
All	54.9	13.2	25.6	6.3
White	66.7	9.5	18.7	5.2
Pakistani	33.3	27.8	31.5	7.4
Bangladeshi	33.3	8.3	50.0	8.3
Indian				
(N = 70)	26.2	19.0	45.2	9.5
(N = 65)	40.0	10.0	40.0	10.0
Male	69.3	13.6	14.5	2.6
Female	43.8	10.8	35.1	10.3

χ^2 across ethnic groups = 54.660 ($p<0.01$)
χ^2 across gender   = 41.002 ($p<0.01$)

TABLE 7.14 *Sources of help in passing examinations by sex and ethnic group*
(shown as percentages)

Source	All	White	Pakistani	Bangladeshi	Indian	West Indian	Male	Female
Teachers	79.8	74.6	84.7	86.7	83.3	77.8	74.9	85.6
Parents	63.4	59.8	67.8	73.3	54.8	44.4	61.4	65.7
Other pupils	17.2	16.7	11.9	13.3	23.8	11.0	16.7	17.7
Friends outside school	14.4	11.7	20.3	20.0	19.0	11.0	13.0	6.0
The school	23.5	18.6	23.7	20.0	46.6	11.0	22.8	24.3
Brothers and sisters	59.6	57.2	67.2	66.7	50.0	77.8	61.4	57.5
Others	2.0	2.3	–	–	–	–	1.4	2.8

$\chi^2 = 20.8, p = 0.002$

TABLE 7.15 *Sources of hindrance in passing examinations by sex and ethnic group*
(shown as percentages)

Source	All	White	Pakistani	Bangladeshi	Indian	West Indian	Male	Female
Teachers	8.6	7.7	8.9	20.0	5.0	–	9.5	7.5
Parents	4.3	3.1	3.6	13.3	5.0	6.5	3.2	5.6
Other pupils	70.2	65.5	55.4	60.0	55.0	25.0	72.5	67.5
Friends outside school	37.5	32.2	32.1	46.7	32.5	37.5	33.9	41.9
The school	6.0	5.0	5.4	13.3	2.5	–	4.2	8.1
Brothers and sisters	28.9	29.1	14.3	20.0	17.5	62.5	24.9	33.7
Others	4.6	3.4	1.8	13.3	7.5	5.0	4.2	5.0

$\chi^2 = 14.29, p = 0.026$

TABLE 7.16	*Father's interest as perceived by the youngster according to ethnic group and sex*
(shown as percentages)

	A great deal	A fair amount	Some	A little	None at all
All	45.7	3.9	11.7	6.0	5.7
White	47.9	30.2	11.7	4.8	5.4
Pakistani	49.8	26.0	14.9	5.6	3.7
Bangladeshi	40.0	20.0	20.0	6.7	13.3
Indian	42.5	38.1	6.9	6.9	4.6
West Indian	35.0	30.0	10.0	20.0	5.0
Male	41.2	33.3	14.4	6.9	4.2
Female	51.5	27.8	8.3	4.7	7.7

χ^2 across ethnic groups = 27.279 ($p = 0.291$)
χ^2 across sex	= 8.950 ($p = 0.0623$)

TABLE 7.17	*Mother's interest as perceived by the youngster according to ethnic group and sex*
(shown as percentages)

	A great deal	A fair amount	Some	A little	None at all
All	58.4	30.1	7.3	1.8	2.5
White	59.7	31.4	5.8	1.2	1.9
Pakistani	61.1	24.1	9.3	3.7	1.9
Bangladeshi	46.7	40.0	6.7	–	6.7
Indian	47.6	33.3	11.9	2.4	4.8
West Indian	65.0	15.0	15.0	5.0	–
Male	53.9	32.4	10.5	1.4	1.8
Female	63.9	27.2	3.3	2.2	3.3

χ^2 across ethnic groups = 27.073 ($p = 0.3010$)
χ^2 across sex	= 10.872 ($p = 0.0280$)

TABLE 7.18 *Correlation of pupils' and their parents' aspirations*

	A and B	A and C	B and C
All	0.0608	0.8414***	0.1445*
White	0.0641	0.3005***	0.1027
Pakistani	0.1170	0.7943***	0.1217
Bangladeshi	0.6508**	0.9262***	0.8973**
Indian	0.0197	0.9161***	0.1331
West Indian	0.1369	0.8321***	0.6468*
Males	0.0555	0.7343***	0.2093*
Females	0.0587	0.9011***	0.0970

A = Pupil's vocational aspiration   * 5% significance
B = Paternal vocational aspiration   ** 1% significance
C = Maternal vocational aspiration   *** 0.1% significance

TABLE 7.19 *Sources of information about jobs by ethnic group and sex (shown as percentages)*

	Careers Officer	Family/ parents	Friends	School/ teachers	Media	Others
All	35.6	64.4	33.8	53.6	14.1	6.4
White	31.4	69.7	33.3	48.9	14.4	7.2
Pakistani	39.7	41.4	32.8	50.0	13.8	3.4
Bangladeshi	33.3	46.7	26.7	60.0	13.3	6.7
Indian	34.9	44.2	34.9	58.1	14.0	4.7
West Indian	35.0	53.4	13.5	60.0	5.0	5.0
Male	32.8	59.1	30.2	44.9	14.2	6.2
Female	36.1	64.3	34.6	57.3	12.4	7.5

TABLE 7.20 *Perceived sources of help in obtaining employment by ethnic group and sex*

	All	White	Pakistani	Bangladeshi	Indian	West Indian	Male	Female
Parental advice	77.3	74.1	89.3	80.0	83.7	68.4	74.8	78.9
Knowing the 'right' people	37.1	42.6	19.6	33.3	27.9	36.8	43.2	29.2
Being clever	23.7	23.6	14.3	33.3	39.5	15.8	23.4	23.2
Being a nice person	56.6	60.1	37.5	53.3	58.1	63.2	47.7	64.9
Good school record	71.7	69.2	73.2	66.7	81.4	84.2	66.2	76.8
Good careers advice	44.9	42.6	39.3	46.7	58.1	63.2	39.6	50.3
Parental help	43.4	42.6	44.6	60.0	63.2	57.9	40.5	45.4

TABLE 7.21 *Mean percentage of total self-esteem from sub-scales by ethnic group and sex*

	General–self	Social–self–peers	Home–parents	School–academic
All	54.203	17.686	15.673	12.439
White	54.609	17.846	15.508	12.023
Pakistani	53.809	17.377	16.072	12.750
Bangladeshi	53.401	15.647	16.400	14.552
Indian	51.998	17.695	16.171	14.135
West Indian	54.905	18.502	15.854	10.738
Male	55.420	17.079	15.314	12.087
Female	52.579	18.434	16.115	12.872

TABLE 7.22   *Analysis of variance summary table for effects on total self-esteem of ethnic group: sex, unemployment and job-direction*

Source	Sum of squares	Degrees of freedom	Mean square	F	p
Ethnic Group (EG)	146.215	1	146.215	6.967	0.016
Sex (S)	4.919	1	4.919	0.234	0.634
Unemployment (U)	248.273	1	248.273	11.830	0.003
Job-Direction (JD)	254.715	1	254.715	12.137	0.002
EG × U	3.390	1	3.390	0.162	0.692
EG × S	40.198	1	40.198	9.195	0.182
U × S	20.351	1	20.351	0.970	0.337
S × JD	15.235	1	15.235	0.726	0.404
EG × U × S	1.607	1	1.607	0.077	0.785
Error	419.724	20	20.986		
Total	829.867	29	23.616		

$F = 8.716, p = 0.003$

TABLE 7.23   *Analysis of variance summary table: school–academic self-esteem by status, sex and ethnic group*

Source of variance	Sum of squares	Degrees of freedom	Mean square	F	p
Sex	0.609	1	0.609	0.056	0.814
Status	66.813	2	33.407	3.078	0.053
Ethnic group	150.450	4	37.612	3.465	0.013
Sex × status	23.245	2	11.773	1.085	0.344
Ethnic group × sex	23.736	3	7.912	0.729	0.539
Ethnic group × status	59.643	7	8.520	0.785	0.602
Ethnic group × sex × status	34.314	4	8.578	0.790	0.536
Error	673.004	62	10.855		
Total	993.349	85	11.689		

TABLE 7.24   *Analysis of variance summary table: social–self–peers self-esteem by status, sex and ethnic group*

Source of variance	Sum of squares	Degrees of freedom	Mean square	F	p
Sex	0.092	1	0.092	0.014	0.906
Status	44.190	2	22.095	3.382	0.040
Ethnic group	22.526	4	5.631	0.862	0.492
Sex × status	27.671	2	13.836	2.118	0.129
Ethnic group × sex	55.924	3	18.641	2.854	0.044
Ethnic group × status	34.126	7	4.875	0.746	0.634
Ethnic group × sex × status	28.057	4	7.014	1.074	0.377
Error	405.029	62	6.533		
Total	622.140	85	7.319		

TABLE 7.25   *Analysis of variance summary table: home–parents self-esteem by status, sex and ethnic group*

Source of variance	Sum of squares	Degrees of freedom	Mean square	F	p
Sex	5.085	1	5.085	0.611	0.437
Status	33.614	2	16.807	2.020	0.141
Ethnic group	26.800	4	6.700	0.805	0.526
Sex × status	35.360	2	17.680	2.125	0.128
Ethnic group × sex	32.778	3	10.926	1.313	0.278
Ethnic group × status	70.609	7	10.087	1.213	0.309
Ethnic group × sex × status	72.509	4	18.127	2.179	0.082
Error	515.759	62	8.319		
Total	821.023	85	9.659		

TABLE 7.26   *Analysis of variance summary table: total self-esteem by status, sex and ethnic group*

Source of variance	Sum of squares	Degrees of freedom	Mean square	F	p
Sex	19.339	1	19.339	0.232	0.631
Status	978.440	2	489.220	5.878	0.005
Ethnic group	247.101	4	61.775	0.742	0.567
Sex × status	418.930	2	209.465	2.517	0.089
Ethnic group × sex	633.251	3	211.085	2.536	0.065
Ethnic group × status	1102.515	7	157.502	1.892	0.086
Ethnic group × sex × status	700.595	4	175.149	2.104	0.091
Error	5160.265	62	83.230		
Total	9355.953	85	110.070		

Appendix 2:   The Pupil Interview Schedule

STAGE 1

This consists of establishing factual variables, which are frequently poorly translated onto questionnaires.

(a) Ethnic Origin

(i) 1st Generation ☐ 1
   2nd Generation (or longer) ☐ 2

(ii) White British ☐ 1
   Irish ☐ 2
   East European ☐ 3
   West Indian ☐ 4
   African ☐ 5
   Punjabi Sikh ☐ 6
   Other Indian ☐ 7
   East African Asian ☐ 8
   Pakistani ☐ 9
   Bangladeshi ☐ 10
   Other ☐ 11

(iii) Mixed marriage?   Yes ☐ 1
                                          No ☐ 2

(b) Geographical Area of Settlement

(i) Type of household (dominant type in neighbourhood)

   Council house/flat ☐ 1
   Non-Council rented house/flat ☐ 2
   Owner occupied house/flat ☐ 3

(ii) Age and condition of housing:

Modern (1950+) good condition	☐ 1
Modern (1950+) poor condition	☐ 2
Inter-war good condition	☐ 3
Inter-war poor condition	☐ 4
Victorian good condition	☐ 5
Victorian poor condition	☐ 6

(iii) Estimated level of ethnic concentration

"The proportion of Asians living in the streets near me is about ...."

20%–30%	☐ 1
10%–20%	☐ 2
5%–10%	☐ 3
0%–5%	☐ 4

"The proportion of West Indians living in the streets near me is about ...."

20%–30%	☐ 1
10%–20%	☐ 2
5%–10%	☐ 3
0%–5%	☐ 4

(c) Length of stay in Britain

....

(d) Amount of schooling abroad (please specify)

....

....

(e) Family size

Mother
Father
Brothers
Sisters

(f) Father's job

....

Social class ⬜ Socio-economic group ⬜

(g) Mother's job

....

Social class ⬜ Socio-economic group ⬜

(h) Other employed members of family

Brothers' jobs 1. ....

2. ....

3. ....

Sisters' jobs 1. ....

2. ....

3. ....

(i) Language used at home/second language

Urdu	☐	1
Punjabi	☐	2
Gujerati	☐	3
Hindi	☐	4
Bengali	☐	5
Other	☐	6

(j) Reads a newspaper? Give the name

Local	☐	1
National quality	☐	2
National tabloid	☐	3

(k) Looks at job advertisements?

Yes	☐	1
No	☐	2

(l) How much careers teaching at school?

(m) Opinion of careers teaching?

(n) Length of careers interview?

(o) Opinion of careers interview

(p) What would you like to see included in careers education?

(q) Were you ever told about:

The wages/salary for the job you wanted?
How to do well in an interview?
Registering as unemployed?

(r) Has your school ever organised work experience or a link course in your field of interest?

STAGE 2 (turn on tape recorder)

I want you to think back now, and try to remember when you first started thinking about getting a job. When was that?

Can you remember what made you start thinking about it?

Have your parents ever given you any encouragement or advice about jobs?
(PROBE for details)

Have they ever had any particular ideas about what you should do?

Do either or both your parents work?

What do you think of the sort(s) of job(s) they do?

Do *they* seem to enjoy their work?

Do they have any friendships based on the workplace? Do you think that this is
something you might enjoy about work?

Do you think it is more important that a job:

>   Should help you to get on/achieve status?
>   Should just pay quite well?
>   Allow for a lot of free time?

Assuming you can only choose one, what sort of job would you *like*?
(EXPAND – why would they like it etc.)

What sort of job do you *expect*? (again – EXPAND reasons)

  (i) Do you know much about what this job involves? For instance, could
       you describe to me how you would spend your working day? (if they
       have chosen college, ask which course and why)
 (ii) Do you know how well it pays?
(iii) Do you have any idea how easy or difficult these jobs are to come by?
       PROBE – (1) ideas regarding necessary qualifications;
                 (2) ideas regarding extent of competition.
 (iv) Bearing these factors in mind do you think that you are likely to get the
       job that you want? It would be a good idea to probe here the extent of
       the individual's determination to obtain this job, or class of job by any
       means whatever.

What sort of job would you like if you have an absolutely free choice?

What sort of person would you like to be?

Is it important in your immediate circle of friends, relatives (community) that
you get a good job?

How good a job?

(FOR ASPIRERS)
To achieve a good career you have to work hard at school. Do you enjoy this
work, or do you just feel there is pressure on you to do it?

What will you do if you don't get the qualifications that you need to get the job
you want?

What is your ideal future?

Would you mind having another chat with me about this on another occasion –
and with your parents perhaps?

On the questionnaire which we gave you before, there was one question which asked whether you had wanted different sorts of jobs earlier in your life. Could you tell me now if that is true. For instance, did you think of something when you were eleven, like being a footballer, or a nurse, or a lorry driver, or anything which you no longer think of doing?

Why did you stop thinking about that job?

Could you tell me what you think your school life has had to do with your choice of working life in the future?

Could you just describe for me how you see things happening from now on?

What sort of activity would you like to do in your spare time?

Finally, I'd like you to spend a few minutes talking to me about two sorts of things. Firstly, what sort of things do you think help you to get on in life? Secondly, what are the sorts of things that hold you back? Think of as many as you like. (Elaborate if necessary)

Appendix 3: Pupil Questionnaire

School ....

Form ....

Date of Birth ....

Boy or Girl ....

This is not a test or an exam. It is a series of questions to find out something about yourself and your opinions. Please complete all the questions as carefully as possible. If, for some good reason, you cannot or do not want to answer a particular question then leave it and pass on to the next question. If there is something you do not understand then put your hand up and we shall explain it more fully.

Thank you for your help.

....

Please mark the appropriate boxes.

1. Where were you born?

    Britain ☐
    Pakistan ☐
    Bangladesh ☐
    India ☐
    West Indies ☐
    Africa ☐
    Other (Please state) ☐

Please do not write in this margin

....

2. Where were your Mother and Father born?

	Mother	Father
Britain	☐	☐
Pakistan	☐	☐
Bangladesh	☐	☐
India	☐	☐
West Indies	☐	☐
Africa	☐	☐
Other (Please state)	☐	☐

....

3. Are your Mother and Father both alive?

Father   Yes   ☐
             No
Mother   Yes
             No   ☐

4. Do you speak any language(s) other than English? If so, which?

....

5. Which language do you normally speak at home?

....

6. When do you expect to leave school?

1984 Easter   ☐
1984 Summer
1985
1986   ☐

7. How many exams are you expecting to take at the end of the year?

Number of GCEs   ☐
Number of CSEs
Other exams (Please state)   ☐

....
....

8. How much do you think success in these exams will help you to get a job?

A great deal   ☐
A fair amount
Some
A little
Not at all   ☐

8a. Why do you think so? Give brief reasons.

....

....

....

....

_____ _____

9. What do you intend to do when you leave school?

Get a job ☐
Go to University ☐
Go to a Polytechnic ☐
Got to a College of Further
  Education (like Bradford College) ☐
Other (Please state)

....

_____ _____

10. What do you hope to do when you complete your education?

....

_____ _____

10a. Why? Please give brief reasons.

....

....

....

....

_____ _____

11. How hard do you think it will be to get this job?

Very easy ☐
Easy ☐
Difficult ☐
Very difficult ☐
Not sure ☐

_____ _____

11a. Why do you think so? Please give brief reasons?

....

....

....

....

_____ _____

12. Do you think you will get this job?

Yes ☐
No ☐

_____ _____

12a. If your answer is NO, what job do you think you will get?

....

_____ _____

13. What is your Father's job?

....

_____ _____

13a. What job do you think your Father would like you to do when you complete your education?

....

_____ _____

13b. How much interest do you think your Father takes in your education and future career?

      A great deal
      A fair amount
      Some
      A little
      None at all

_____ _____

14. What is your Mother's job? (If she works outside the home, if not please write 'housewife')

....

_____ _____

14a. What job do you think your Mother would like you to do when you complete your education?

....

_____ _____

14b. How much interest do you think your Mother takes in your education and future career?

      A great deal
      A fair amount
      Some
      A little
      None at all

_____ _____

15. When did you decide what job you would like to do?

      Not yet decided
      This term
      Last term
      Last year
      2 years ago
      More than 2 years ago

_____ _____

16. How much do you know about the job which you want to do when you complete your education?

      Everything ☐
      Quite a lot ☐
      Just enough ☐
      A little bit ☐
      Nothing ☐   ____ ____

17. If you wanted to know more about this job who would you ask? Or where would you look?

....

....   ____ ____

18. Which of the following people/places have already given you information about jobs? (Please mark *all* those appropriate).

      Parents and family ☐
      Friends ☐
      Teachers/School ☐
      Radio/Television/Newspapers ☐
      Bradford Careers Office ☐
      Other (Please state) ☐

      ....   ____ ____

19. How much do you worry about getting a job when complete your education?

      A great deal ☐
      A fair amount ☐
      Some ☐
      A little ☐
      Not at all ☐   ____ ____

19a. Why? Please give brief reasons.

      ....

      ....

      ....   ____ ____

20. Which of the following do you think help someone to get a job? (Please mark *all* those appropriate)

      Passing exams ☐
      Knowing the right people ☐
      Being clever ☐
      Being a nice person ☐
      Having a good school record ☐
      Good careers advice ☐
      Help from your parents ☐   ____ ____

21. Would you be willing to work away from Bradford if necessary?

    Yes
    No

22. Who out of the following do you think help you to do well at school? (Please mark *all* those appropriate)

    Teachers
    Parents
    Other pupils
    Friends outside school
    Brothers and sisters
    Yourself
    Others (Please state)

    ....

22a. Why do you think so? Please give brief reasons.

    ....
    ....
    ....

23. Who out of the following do you think stop you from doing better at school? (Please mark *all* those appropriate)

    Teachers
    Parents
    Other pupils
    Friends outside school
    Brothers and sisters
    Yourself
    Others (Please state)

    ....

23a. Why do you think so? Please give brief reasons.

    ....
    ....
    ....
    ....

24.   If when you leave school, you can't find a job, who
      do you think would be to blame? (Please mark *all*
      those appropriate)

       Yourself
       Friends
       Parents
       Teachers
       The Government
       Employers
       Others (Please state)

....

24a. Why do you think so? Please give brief reasons.

....
....
....

25.   If for some reason you do not pass the exams you
      are taking, what will you do?

       Retake exams at school
       Retake exams somewhere else
       Not retake
       Don't know

26.   Since last September, how many times have you
      been away from school?

       None
       Once or twice
       3–10 times
       10–20 times
       Over 20 times

27.   On the whole, how much do you enjoy going to
      school?

       A great deal
       A fair amount
       Some
       A little
       Not at all

28. Please describe briefly what you do in your spare time.

   ....

   ....

   ....

   ....

    _____ _____

29. Which of the following statements best fits what you think about filling in this questionnaire?

       I disliked it a lot

       I disliked it a bit

       Indifferent

       I liked it a bit

       I liked it a lot

    _____ _____

29a. Why do you think so? Please give your reasons.

   ....

   ....

   ....

   ....

    _____ _____

Appendix 4:   The Interview Schedule

TO BE FILLED IN BY INTERVIEWER

DATE ....

SCHOOL/SCHOOLS ATTENDED ....
....

NAME OF INTERVIEWEE ....
....

ADDRESS ....

TYPE OF HOUSING – TERRACE ....
                     FLATS ....
                     SEMI ....
                     DETACHED ....
                     OTHER ....

COMMENTS ON:

  (i) Openness of interviewee ....
....

 (ii) Attitude towards question ....
....

(iii) Overt parental influence ....
....

(iv) Other ....
....

INTERVIEW SCHEDULE

(A) ETHNIC ORIGIN
     (i) Have you lived in Britain all your life?
    (ii) Have your parents lived in Britain all their lives?
   (iii) How long have you lived in in Britain?
    (iv) Where were you (your parents) born?
    (v) Mixed marriage?

(B) OWN JOB ....

(C) FATHER'S JOB ....

(D) MOTHER'S JOB ....
(E) OTHER MEMBERS OF FAMILY (NUCLEAR) ....
....
....
....
....
....

(F) JOB HISTORY

	From	To	Job	Reason why left
1.	....	....	....	....
2.	....	....	....	....
3.	....	....	....	....
4.	....	....	....	....

(G) SIZE OF PRESENT EMPLOYER .... (No. of employees)

(H) TIME SINCE LAST EMPLOYMENT ....

(I) AMOUNT OF SCHOOLING ABROAD ....

(J) DATE ON LEAVING SCHOOL ....
(K) APPROXIMATE NUMBER OF INTERVIEWS BEFORE OBTAINING EMPLOYMENT (OR TO DATE) ....

(L) HOW PRESENT EMPLOYMENT WAS OBTAINED:

1. Through the Careers Service ....
2. Parental help ....
3. Relatives/friends help ....
4. In response to newspaper advertisement ....
5. Called personally at place of work ....
6. Through own initiative ....
7. Job Centre ....
8. School help ....
9. Other ....

SECTION TWO – SWITCH ON TAPE

1. What job opportunities do you think Bradford/Leeds holds for you?
2. What are your chances of getting a better job?

3. How satisfied are you with your present job? (Expand reasons)

4. Are your parents satisfied with your present job?

5. Are you given day release or other time for studying? (Expand)

6. What sort of jobs are you looking for, and why?

OPTIONAL QUESTIONS (PLEASE ASK INTERVIEWEE FOR PERMISSION TO TALK ABOUT THESE MATTERS)

7. Present income .... per week.

8. Are you satisfied with your present income? ....
....

9. Do you have any political affiliation? (Expand) ....
....

10. Are you a member of a Trade Union? ....
....

11. Have you ever been refused a job because of your ethnic origin, skin colour etc? ....

12. Does your religion prevent you from taking on certain jobs? ....
....

13. Do you think that some employers discriminate on racial/ethnic grounds? ....

14. What were your reasons for going to college/university? (Expand) ....
....

15. Would you be willing to move to another part of the country in order to get a job? ....

16. Do you think that it is more important that a job:
    (a) Should help you to 'get on'/achieve status
    (b) Should pay quite well
    (c) Allow for a lot of free time

17. How do you think your schooling affected your ideas on educational success/job importance? ....

18. Do you think that the careers teaching at school helped you to adjust to working life? ....

19. Where would you like to go, in terms of jobs, from your present situation? What is your ideal future? ....

20. If, by some bad luck, you were made redundant, how hard do you think it would be to get another job? ....

21. How do you spend your spare time? ....
....

22. Do you ever intend to return to your (your parents') country of birth? .....

23. Finally, I should like you to spend a few minutes talking to me about two
    sorts of things. Firstly, what sort of things do you think help you to get on
    in life, secondly what are the sort of things which hold you back? Think of
    as many as you like.

....
....
....
....
....
....
....

Appendix 5: Summary of the Findings of Chapters Seven and Eight

The summary presented here attempts to draw together the findings presented in both Chapters Seven and Eight. In order that the general tenor of the findings may be better absorbed, they have been presented under a series of topic headings. As a result, some caution should be exercised when reading them, since they should be read within the full context of the study.

GENERAL

1. Ethnic minority young people suffer from many educational and social disadvantages.
2. The struggle for social mobility on the part of ethnic minority groups is closely bound up with many social, educational and institutional factors which impose numerous disadvantages upon them.
3. Among the most disadvantaged sections particularly there was evidence that ethnic minority youngsters are becoming more and more alienated from school and society at large.
4. Educational achievement *or* lack thereof cannot be attributed to one single factor.
5. No single factor was found to differentiate between ethnic groups in terms of educational achievement.
6. A combination of factors contributed in *different* ways and with varying degrees of importance for the ethnic groups featuring in this study. Although ethnic minority youngsters were studied in terms of differing ethnicities, this represented, nonetheless, a crude differentiation between those youngsters. The cultural experience of each youngster is likely to be *unique*; this study has, however, attempted to advance the study of the problems and issues relating to educational achievement beyond the cruder measures employed in earlier studies.

SCHOOL

7. The biased school curriculum, racial discrimination and the current unemployment situation contributed to a large extent to the failure among West Indian and Asian youngsters to find work.
8. Among the most disadvantaged sections particularly there was evidence that ethnic minority youngsters are becoming more and more alienated from school and society at large.
9. School was a major influence on pupil achievement. Contributory factors included:

   – teachers' stereotyped attitudes and antipathy towards pupils from the ethnic minorities;
   – racial prejudice among teachers;
   – prejudice among white pupils against West Indians and Asians;
   – poor school discipline, resulting in lack of motivation and poor performance;
   – the school was held responsible for poor achievement by approximately half of the youngsters in the sample.

10. The school was also a major influence on the achievement of youngsters, both in terms of passing examinations and looking for employment. The nature and extent of the influence depends largely on the characteristics of the individual.
11. Careers teaching in secondary schools was not only inadequate and unhelpful but, in many cases, the careers interview was devoted mainly to disabusing ethnic minority pupils of *unreasonable* aspirations. In other words, careers advice is often biased.
12. Contemplating the prospect of finding it difficult to obtain jobs, South Asian youngsters tended to give 'internalised' reasons – e.g. it would be the result of their failure to obtain proper qualifications whereas white and West Indian youngsters tended to give 'externalised' reasons – e.g. it would be the result of the depressed labour market.

TEACHERS

13. Our research found that there was discrimination and prejudice on the part of a significant number of teachers and employers.
14. In their ordinary classroom interactions teachers often operate on the basis of stereotypes, naïve assumptions and self-fulfilling prophesies. It was also noted that many teachers held unconscious stereotyped views of ethnic minority pupils.
15. Addiction to the assimilationist position leads many teachers to ignore the reality of the cultural, social and personal aspirations of ethnic minority pupils.

SCHOOL TO WORK

16. The majority of young people from ethnic minority groups found

difficulties of various kinds in their transition from school to work/further education.

17. South Asian and West Indian youngsters used 'formal' networks when seeking employment or entry to Higher Education; white youngsters often used 'informal' networks, e.g. family, relatives, friends of family.

18. Unemployment was higher for South Asian and West Indian school-leavers than for whites.

19. 'Underemployment' among South Asian youngsters was higher than among their white counterparts.

20. Contemplating the prospect of finding it difficult to obtain jobs, South Asian youngsters tended to give 'internalised' reasons – e.g. it would be the result of their failure to obtain proper qualifications – whereas white and West Indian youngsters tended to give 'externalised' reasons – e.g. it would be the result of the depressed labour market.

ACHIEVEMENT

21. It is clear from our study that achievement is culture-based.

22. The antecedents of educational achievement were different between ethnic groups.

23. Socio-economic factors also contribute to the educational achievement of pupils.

PARENTS/FAMILY

24. It is clear from our study that educational achievement is culture-based.

25. Family structure/styles played a significant part in the achievement process.

26. Parents are the major source of motivation in the educational achievement process:

    – maternal influence was greater than paternal influence, particularly for West Indian and Pakistani youngsters;
    – West Indian youngsters tended to mention their mother as being the major influence upon them; South Asian parents tended to give more advice or direct guidance to their children.

YOUNGSTERS

27. The school is a major influence on the achievement of youngsters, both in terms of passing examinations and looking for employment. The nature and extent of the influence depends largely on the characteristics of the individual.

28. Contemplating the prospect of finding it difficult to obtain jobs, South Asian youngsters tended to give 'internalised' reasons – e.g. it would be the result of their failure to obtain proper qualifications – whereas white

and West Indian youngsters tended to give 'externalised' reasons – e.g. it would be the result of the depressed labour market.

29. West Indian and Asian youngers experience increasing frustration and alienation through failure to obtain their goal of economic and social mobility.

30. Some South Asian youngsters felt somewhat confused about their cultural identity; some rejected the traditional parental values, others were firm in sticking to those values.

31. Second and third generation descendants of the original migrants are becoming more sophisticated in their educational and occupational orientations. In this they appear to be learning from their white peers.

32. White youngsters expect cultural change to work in one direction: i.e. 'immigrants' should adopt the values of the indigenous culture.

SELF-ESTEEM

33. It is clear from our research that, contrary to many studies, the level of youngsters' self-esteem is not affected by the individual's ethnicity.

34. Self-esteem is an important factor in the achievement process for West Indians but not for Asians. However, enhancement of self-esteem for West Indians is derived from the peer group; the school played a smaller part.

35. South Asian youngsters derived a greater part of their self-esteem from school, except for the Bangladeshis, who derived their self-esteem from the home.

36. White youngsters had higher self-esteem than West Indians and South Asians.

References

Acton, T. A. (1981) 'Educational Criteria of Success: Some Problems in the Work of Rutter, Maughan, Mortinore and Ouston', *Educational Research*, 22, 3, 163–9.

Adorno, T. W. *et al.* (1950) *The Authoritarian Personality*, New York: Harper.

Allport, G. W. (1958) *The Nature of Prejudice*, New York: Doubleday Anchor Books.

Anwar, M. (1979) *The Myth of Return: Pakistanis in Britain*, London: Heinemann.

Appleton, N. (1983) *Cultural Pluralism in Education: Theoretical Foundations*, New York: Longman.

Arensberg, C. and Niehoff, A. (1971) *Introducing Social Change*, Chicago: Aldine & Atherton.

Argyle, M. and Robinson, P. (1962) 'Two Origins of Achievement Motivation' *British Journal of Social and Clinical Psychology*, 107–20.

Ashworth, B. J. (1983) *Careers Education: Some Dimensions and Perspectives in a Multicultural Society*, unpublished M.Phil. Thesis: University of Bradford.

Atkinson, J. W. (1958) (ed.) *Motives in Fantasy, Action and Society*, New York: Van Nostrad.

Ausubel, D. P. (1958) 'Ego Development among Segregated Negro Children', *Mental Hygiene* 42, 362–9.

Bagley, C. (1973) *The Dutch Plural Society: A Comparative Study in Race Relations*, London: Oxford University Press.

Bagley, C. (1979) 'Inter-ethnic Marriage in Britain and the United States from 1970–77', *Sage Race Relations Abstract* 4, 1–22.

Bagley, C., Bart, M. and Wong, J. (1979) 'Antecedents of Scholastic Success in West Indian ten-year-olds in London', in G. Verma and C. Bagley (eds) *Race, Education and Identity*, London: Macmillan.

Bagley, C., Mallick, K. and Verma, G. K. (1979) 'Pupil Self-esteem: A Study of Black and White Teenagers in British Schools', in G. Verma and C. Bagley (eds) *Race, Education and Identity*, London: Macmillan.

Bagley, C. and Verma, G. K. (1979) *Racial Prejudice, the Individual and Society*, Farnborough, England: Saxon House.

Bagley, C. and Verma, G. K. (1983) (eds) *Multicultural Childhood: Education, Ethnicity and Cognitive Styles*, Aldershot, England: Gower Publishing.

Bagley, C. and Verma, G. K. (1983) 'Introduction: Issues in Multicultural Education', in C. Bagley and G. K. Verma (eds) *Multicultural Childhood:*

Education, Ethnicity and Cognitive Styles, Aldershot, England: Gower Publishing.

Bagley, C., Verma, G. K., Mallick, K. and Young, L. (1979) *Personality, Self-esteem and Prejudice*, Farnborough, England: Saxon House.

Bagley, C. and Young, L. (1984) 'The Welfare & Identity of Children from Intracultural Marriage' in G. K. Verma and C. Bagley (eds) *Race Relations & Cultural Differences*, London: Croom Helm.

Baker, A. (1978) 'Asians are Not All Alike', *New Society*, 2 November 1978.

Banks, O. (1968) *The Sociology of Education*, London: Batsford.

Banton, M. (1979) 'The Idea of Race and Concept of Race', in G. K. Verma and C. Bagley (eds) *Race, Education and Identity*, London: Macmillan.

Beetham, D. (1967) *Immigrant School-leavers and the Youth Employment Service in Birmingham*, London: Institute of Race Relations.

Brody, E. (1969) 'Migration and Adaptation', in E. Brody (ed.) *Behaviour in New Environments*, Beverly Hills: Sage.

Bradford Metropolitan District Council (1982) *District Trends*, Bradford.

Bradford Metropolitan District Council (1984) *District Trends*, Bradford.

Bradford Metropolitan District Council (1984) *Bradford in Figures*, Bradford.

Brimer, M. A., and Gross, H. (1977) *Wide-span Reading Test*, London: Nelson.

Bullivant, B. (1981) *The Pluralist Dilemma in Education: Six Case Studies*, London: Allen & Unwin.

Cherry, N. M. (1981) 'Ability, Education and Occupational Functioning', in A. G. Watts, D. E. Super and J. M. Kidd (eds) *Career Development in Britain*, London: Hobson Press/Careers Research & Advice Council.

Clarke, A. S. (1974) 'An Analysis of Student's Self-esteem and Student's Attitudes Towards Culture in Secondary Schools in Trinidad', *Dissertation Abstracts International* 34(12-A) 1.

Clark, R. A., Teevan, R. and Riccuitti, H. N. (1956) 'Hope of Success and Fear of Failure as Aspects of Need for Achievement', *Journal of Abnormal and Social Psychology* 53, 182–6.

Coard, B. (1971) *How the West Indian Child is made Educationally Subnormal by the British Education System*, London: New Beacon.

Coleman, J. S. et al. (1966) *Equality of Educational Opportunity*, Washington D.C.: Government Printing Office.

Coleman, J., Hartzberg, J. and Norris, M. (1977) 'Identity in Adolescence: Present and Future Self-concepts', *Journal of Youth and Adolescence*, 6, 63–75.

Collins, R. (1979) *The Credential Society*, London: Academic Press.

Commission for Racial Equality (1978) *Looking for Work: Black and White School-Leavers in Lewisham*, London: Commission for Racial Equality.

Commission for Racial Equality (1980) *Black Unemployment in Britain*, London: Commission for Racial Equality.

Coopersmith, S. (1967) *The Antecedents of Self-Esteem*, San Francisco: Freeman.

Coopersmith, S. (1975) 'Self-concept, Race and Education', in G. K. Verma and C. Bagley (eds) *Race and Education Across Cultures*, London: Heinemann.

Cox, D. (1976) 'Will Australia Ever Be a Pluralist Society?' *Migration Action* 1, 5–7.

Craft, M. and Craft, A. Z. (1983) 'The Participation of Ethnic Minority Pupils in Further and Higher Education', *Educational Research*, 25, 10–17.

Craig, D. (1971) 'The use of language by 7-year-old Jamaican children living in contrasting socioeconomic environments', Ph.D. Thesis, University of London.

Cuming, D. (1983) *School Leavers, Qualifications and Employment*, Nottingham: University of Nottingham.

Deakin, N. (1970) *Colour, Citizenship and British Society*, London: Panther Books.

Department of Education and Science (1981) *West Indian Children in our Schools – Interim Report of the Committee of Inquiry into the Education of Children from Ethnic Minority Groups*, London: HMSO (CMND 8273)

Department of Education and Science (1985) *Education for All – The Report of the Committee of Inquiry into the Education of Children from Ethnic Minority Groups*, London: HMSO (CMND 9453)

Department of Education and Science (1967) *Children and their Primary Schools* (The Plowden Report) London: HMSO.

Department of Employment *Gazette* (1972) *List of Key Occupations for Statistical Purposes*, September, pp. 799–802.

Dore, E. (1976) *The Diploma Disease*, London: Unwin Educational.

Driver, G. (1977) 'Cultural Competence, Social Power and School Achievement' *New Community* 5, 353–9.

Driver, G. (1980) *Beyond Underachievement*, London: Commission for Racial Equality.

Dyer, K. (1974) *The Biology of Racial Integration*, Bristol: Scientechnica.

Eysenck, H. (1971) *Race, Intelligence and Education*, London: Temple Smith.

Flynn, J. (1980) *Race, I.Q. and Jensen*, London: Routledge.

Fowler, B., Littlewood, B. and Madigan, R. (1977) 'Immigrant School-leavers and the Search for Work', *Sociology* II, I.

Gipps, C., Steadman, S., Blackstone, T, and Stierer, B. (1983) *Testing Children*, London: Heinemann Educational Books.

Glazer, N. and Moynihan, D. P. (1975) (eds) *Ethnicity: Theory and Experiences*, Cambridge, Mass.: Harvard University Press.

Goldman, P. (1974) *The Death and Life of Malcolm X*, London: Gollancz.

Goldman, R. K. and Mercer, B. (1976) 'Self-esteem and Self-differentiation: A Comparison between Black and White Children in Follow-through, and Non Follow-through Classes', *Educational Research Quarterly*, 1, 3, 43–9.

Gupta, Y. P. (1977) 'The Educational and Vocational Aspirations of Asian Immigrant and English School-leavers', *British Journal of Sociology* 28, 185–98.

Halsey, A. H. and Goldthorpe, D. (1980) *Origins and Destinations: Family, Class and Education in Modern Britain*, Oxford: Oxford University Press.

Heckhausen, H. (1967) *The Anatomy of Achievement Motivation*, New York and London: Academic Press.

Himmelweit, H. T. and Swift, B. (1971) 'Adolescent and Adult Authoritarianism Re-examined', *Journal of European Social Psychology* I, 359–283.

Husen, T. (1979) *The School in Question*, Oxford: Oxford University Press.

Jefferey, P. (1976) *Migrants and Refugees: Muslim and Christian Pakistani Families in Bristol*, Cambridge: Cambridge University Press.

Jelinek, M. and Brittan, E. M. (1975) 'Multi-racial Education I: Inter-ethnic friendship patterns', *Educational Research* 18, 44–53.

Jencks, C. *et al.* (1972) *Inequality: A Reassessment of the Effect of Family and Schooling in America*, New York: Basic Books.

Jensen, A. R. (1969) 'How Much Can We Boost I.Q. and Scholastic Achievement?' *Harvard Educational Review*, 39, 1–123.

Jensen, A. R. (1973) *Educability and Group Differences*, London: Methuen.

Korman, A. K. (1966) 'Self-esteem Variable in Vocational Choice', *Journal of Applied Psychology* 50, 6, 479–86.

Korman, A. K. (1970) 'Towards an Hypothesis of Work Behaviour', *Journal of Applied Psychology* 54, 1, 31–4.

Labenne, W. and Greene, B. (1969) *Educational Implications of Self-Concept Theory*, California: Goodyear.

Laferriere, M. (1983) 'Racism in Education: Old and New', in R. Douglas and D'Oyley (eds) *Human Rights in Canadian Education*, Dubugne, Iowa: Kendell & Hunt.

Lewis, M. (1978) *The Culture of Inequality*, New York: Meridian Books.

Little, A. (1978) 'Schools and Race', in *Five Views of Multiracial Britain*, London: Commission for Racial Equality.

Little, A. and Willey, R. (1981) *Multi-Ethnic Education: The Way Forward*, Pamphlet 18, London: Schools Council.

Louden, D. (1978) *A Comparative Study of Self-esteem and Locus of Control in Minority Group Adolescents*, unpublished Ph.D. Thesis, University of Bristol.

McClelland, D. C. *et al.* (1953) *The Achievement Motive*, New York: Appleton – Century Crofts, Inc.

Mackintosh, N. J. and Mascie-Taylor, C. G. N. (1985) 'The I.Q. Question' in C. Bagley and G. K. Verma (eds) *Personality, Cognition and Values*, London: Macmillan.

Mackintosh, N. and Smith, D. (1974) *The Extent of Racial Discrimination in Britain*, London: Political and Economic Planning.

Mawer, O. H. (1960) *Learning Theory and Behavior*, New York: Wiley.

Milner, D. (1975) 'Racial Identification and Preference in Black British Children', *European Journal of Social Psychology* 3, 281–95.

Montagu, A. (1977) 'On the Non-perception of "Race" Differences', *Current Anthropology* 18, 743–4.

Mullard, C. (1981) 'The Social Context and Meaning of Multicultural Education', in B. Davies (ed.) *Educational Analysis*, Vol. III, Oxford: Carfax Publishing.

Nash, R. (1973) *Classrooms Observed*, London: Routledge.

Parekh, B. (1978) 'Asians in Britain: Problems or Opportunity?', in *Five Views of Multi-Racial Britain*, London: Commission for Racial Equality.

Pettigrew, T. (1964) *A Profile of the Negro American*, New York: Van Nostrand.

Prendergast, M. and Binder, D. (1975) 'Relationships of Selected Self-concepts and Academic Achievement Measures', *Measurement and Evaluation in Guidance* 8, 92–5.

Priestley, J. B. (1934) *English Journey*, London: Heinemann.

Rex, J. and Tomlinson, S. (1979) *Colonial Immigrants in a British City: A Class Analysis*, London: Routledge.

Richmond, A. (1967) *Post-War Immigrants in Canada*, Toronto: University of Toronto Press.

Robinson, V. (1980) 'The Achievement of Asian Children', *Educational Research* 22, 148–50.

Rosenberg, M. and Simmons, R. (1972) *Black and White Self-Esteem: The Urban School Child*, Washington DC: American Sociological Association.

Runnymede Trust (1981) *Employment, Unemployment and the Black Population*, London: Runnymede Trust.

Rutter, M. *et al.* (1979) *Fifteen Thousand Hours*, London: Open Books.

Scarr, S. (1984) *Race, Social Class and Individual Differences in I.Q.*, London: Lawrence Erlbaum Associates.

Schockley, W. (1972) 'Dysgenics, Geneticity, Raceology', *Phi Delta Kappan*, *Special Supplement* 297–307.

Simon, W. and Simon, M. (1975) 'Self-esteem, Intelligence and Standardised Academic Achievement', *Psychology in the School* 12, 97–9.

Smith, D. J. (1976) *Racial Disadvantage in Britain*, Harmondsworth: Penguin Books.

Smith, D. (1981) *Unemployment and Racial Minorities*, London: Political and Economic Planning, Publications no. 594.

Smolicz, J. (1980) *Culture and Education in a Plural Society*, Adelaide: Curriculum Development Centre.

Stone, M. (1981) *The Education of the Black Child in Britain*, Glasgow: Fontana.

Street-Porter, R. (1978) 'From Immigrant to Briton – The Change in Educational Attitudes' in Unit 12–13 *Race and the Urban Child* (E 361 – Education and the Urban Environment) Milton Keynes: Open University.

Sumner, D. (1971) *Motivation Attitude Intensity Scale*, Windsor: National Foundation for Educational Research.

Sumner, R. (1969) *Administrative Manual and Test–Motivation–Attitude Scale*, Slough: National Foundation for Educational Research.

Super, D. E. (1957) *The Psychology of Careers*, New York: Harper & Row.

Super, D. E. (1981) 'Approaches to Occupational Choice and Career Developments', in A. G. Watts, D. E. Super and J. M. Kidd (eds) *Career Development in Britain*, Cambridge: Hobson Careers Research & Advice Council.

Tajfel, H. (1978) (ed.) *Differential Between Social Groups: Studies in the Psychology of Intergroup Relations*, London: Academic Press.

Taylor, J. H. (1976) *The Half-Way Generation*, Windsor: National Foundation for Educational Research.

Thomas-Hope, E. (1982) 'Identity and Adaptation of Migrants from the

English-speaking Caribbean in Britain and North America', in G. K. Verma and C. Bagley (eds) *Self-concept, Achievement and Multicultural Education*, London: Macmillan.

Tinker, H. (1977) *The Banyan Tree: Overseas Emigrants from India, Pakistan and Bangladesh*, London: Oxford University Press.

Triandis, H. (1976) 'The Future of Pluralism', *Journal of Social Issues* 32, 179–208.

Verma, G. K. (1973) 'A Use of Thematic Apperception to Assess Achievement', *Japanese Psychological Research* 15, 45–50.

Verma, G. K. (1975) 'Inter-group Prejudice and Race Relations', in G. K. Verma and C. Bagley (eds) *Race and Education Across Culture*, London: Heinemann.

Verma, G. K. (1979) 'Attitude Measurement in a Multiethnic Society', *Bulletin of the British Psychological Society* 32, 460–2.

Verma, G. K. (1981) *Problems of Vocational Adaptation of South Asian Adolescents in Britain, with Special Reference to the Role of the School*, unpublished report, University of Bradford.

Verma, G. K. (1982) 'The Problems of Vocational Adaptation of Asian Adolescents in Britain: Some Theoretical and Methodological Issues', in G. K. Verma and C. Bagley (eds) *Self-Concept, Achievement and Multicultural Education*, London: Macmillan.

Verma, G. K. (1983) 'Consciousness, Disadvantage and Opportunity: The Struggle for South Asian Youth in British Society', in C. Bagley and G. K. Verma (eds) *Multicultural Childhood: Education, Ethnicity and Cognitive Styles*, Aldershot, England: Gower Publishing.

Verma, G. K. (1983) 'Multicultural Education: Research Problems in the United Kingdom and Elsewhere', in T. Husen and S. Opper (eds) *Multicultural and Multilingual Education in Immigrant Countries*, Oxford: Pergamon.

Verma, G. K. (1984) 'Multicultural Education: Prelude to Practice', in G. K. Verma and C. Bagley (eds) *Race Relations and Cultural Differences*, London: Croom Helm.

Verma, G. K. (1984) 'Self-esteem and Educational Achievement in Young South Asians in Britain', *Educational and Child Psychology*, 1, 1, 35–45.

Verma, G. K. and Bagley, C. (1979) (eds) *Race, Education and Identity*, London: Macmillan.

Verma, G. K. and Bagley, C. (1982) (eds) *Self-Concept, Achievement and Multicultural Education*, London: Macmillan.

Verma, G. K. and Bagley, C. (1984) (eds) *Race Relations and Cultural Differences*, London: Croom Helm.

Verma, G. K. and Beard, R. (1981) *What is Educational Research? Perspectives on Techniques of Research*, Farnborough, England: Gower Publishing.

Verma, G. K. and Mallick, K. (1978) 'The Growth and Nature of Self-esteem: Attitudes and Feelings in Multiethnic Schools', *The New Era* 59(4) July/August.

Verma, G. K. and Mallick, K. (1982) 'Tests and Testing in a Multiethnic Society', in G. K. Verma and C. Bagley (eds) *Self-Concept, Achievement and Multicultural Education*, London: Macmillan.

Verma, G. K., Mallick, K. and Ashworth, B. J. (1983) 'The Role of Attitude and Experience in the Transition from School to Work in Young South Asians in Britain', in C. Bagley and G. K. Verma (eds) *Multicultural Childhood: Education, Ethnicity and Congitive Styles*, Aldershot, England: Gower Publishing.

Waller, P. (1981) 'Liverpool: Why the Clue to Violence is Economic Not Racial', *The Times*, London, 7 July, p. 12.

Weinland, T. *et al.* (1976) 'Self-concept: A Cross-cultural Study', *Perceptional and Motor Skills* 42, 43–6.

Wells, L. and Marwell, G. (1976) *Self-Esteem: Its Conceptualization and Measurement*, London: Sage.

Willey, R. (1982) *Teaching in Multicultural Britain*, York: Longman, for Schools Council.

Willis, P. (1977) *Learning to Labour*, Farnborough, England: Saxon House.

Author Index

Subject Index